Preschool-K-1
GIANT BASIC SKILLS™
Reading Workbook

Gurcharan Bhambra

Modern Publishing
A Division of Unisystems, Inc.
New York, New York 10022
Series UPC Number: 49610

Cover art by Suzanne Vasilak
Illustrated by Arthur Friedman
Educational Consultant, Shereen Gertel Rutman, M.S.

Copyright © 1997 by Modern Publishing,
a division of Unisystems, Inc.

™Giant Basic Skills Preschool–K–1 Workbook is a trademark
of Modern Publishing, a division of Unisystems, Inc.

Printed in the U.S.A.

2 4 6 8 10 9 7 5 3

TO THE PARENTS

Dear Parents,

By using the Giant Basic Skills Preschool–K–1 Workbooks, you are helping your child build an important connection between home and school. These workbooks have been carefully designed by educators to teach children skills in a developmentally appropriate manner. The activities build on the growing abilities of your child. Each section begins with simple exercises, and the age level increases gradually as children practice and master various skills. With your guidance, children will enjoy working on the activities and gain important learning skills at the same time.

Following are some suggestions to help make your time together enjoyable and rewarding for your child.

- Work on this book when both you and your child are calm, relaxed, and not tired.

- Choose a quiet place to work together.

- Make sure you have the materials you need, such as pencils and crayons or markers.

- Encourage your child to work on activities appropriate to his or her skill level. Each section begins with preschool-level activities and progresses through kindergarten to first grade level.

- Talk about each page and make sure your child understands the directions.

- Work on a few pages at each sitting. Rather than do too much, find ways to extend the activities away from the book.

- Compliment your child's work. Praise will encourage your child to accomplish more.

- Have fun! The time spent working on this book should be enjoyable for you and your child.

ESSENTIAL SKILLS

The repetitive activities within each chapter have been designed to help children learn to sort, separate, put together, and figure out—the organizational skills so necessary for learning and thinking. Activities in each section progress from easiest to most challenging.

CHAPTER 1   Thinking Skills
In this chapter, children follow simple directions to practice skills essential to learning to read, including **identifying colors and shapes, fine motor skills, logical reasoning, visual discrimination, visual memory,** and **recognizing similarities. Spatial awareness** and **knowledge of left and right** are also explored.

CHAPTER 2   Comparing and Classifying
Children learn to make sense of the world by **making comparisons** and **identifying relationships** between things. The exercises in this chapter encourage children to use **logical reasoning skills** as they **identify parts of a whole, recognize pairs,** and **visually match** groups of objects. **Handwriting skills** and **vocabulary recognition** are also employed.

CHAPTER 3   Opposites
As children identify opposites, they **develop vocabulary** and further their **matching skills.** Exercises focus on **recognizing opposites** in groups of words. **Handwriting** and **fine motor skills** are also practiced.

CHAPTER 4   Story Order
This chapter focuses on children's comprehension of **story order.** They are asked to **identify parts of a story** and use **logical reasoning** to **sequence** events.

CHAPTER 5   Rhyming Words
Children use their **auditory discrimination skills** and their ability to **recognize sounds** in this chapter. **Word families** are explored in various ways as children learn to **identify rhyming words.**

CHAPTER 6   Reasoning Skills
This chapter focuses on children's thinking ability. Children use **visual discrimination, logic, knowledge of spatial relations, association skills,** and **inference** to solve problems. Word problems encourage the use of **deductive reasoning.**

CHAPTER 7   Letter Concepts
This section is designed to develop children's knowledge of the alphabet. Exercises include **recognition of uppercase and lowercase letters,** and **fine motor skills** are developed as children practice writing the alphabet.

CHAPTER 8   Phonics
Activities that teach **sound/symbol association** are featured in this chapter. Children use **auditory discrimination skills** to recognize **initial consonants, final consonants,** and **vowel sounds.**

CHAPTER 9   ABC Order
Children use their knowledge of letters to **alphabetize** simple words. **Fine motor skills** and **visual discrimination skills** are enhanced through these exercises.

CHAPTER 10   Shapes and Colors
Fine motor skills and **visual discrimination** are used to **recognize and identify colors and shapes. Color words** and **shape words** are also explored in this chapter.

CHAPTER 11   Words About Numbers
Basic knowledge of numbers is extended as children **recognize numerals and number words.** Children use **fine motor skills** as they practice **writing numerals** and **matching numerals with number words.**

CHAPTER 12   Vocabulary Building
This chapter helps children to broaden their **sight-reading vocabulary. Fine motor skills** and **visual discrimination** are used in activities that emphasize **vocabulary and spelling words.**

CHAPTER 13   Comprehension
The final chapter puts many of the previously learned skills to work. Children use **spelling words** and **sight vocabulary** to read simple sentences. **Comprehension skills** are employed in **following directions.** Children also learn to **complete sentences based on context clues.**

TABLE OF CONTENTS

Thinking Skills 6

Comparing and Classifying. 46

Opposites 87

Story Order 107

Rhyming Words 131

Reasoning Skills 151

Letter Concepts 166

Phonics 187

ABC Order 230

Shapes and Colors 246

Word About Numbers 277

Vocabulary Building 290

Comprehension 304

THINKING SKILLS

Look at the shapes on this page.
Color all the circles green.
Color all the squares blue.
Color all the triangles red.
Color all the rectangles yellow.

Skills: Following directions; Identifying colors and shapes

THINKING SKILLS

Look at the fruits on this page.
Color all the apples red.
Color all the bananas yellow.
Color all the grapes purple.
Color all the oranges orange.

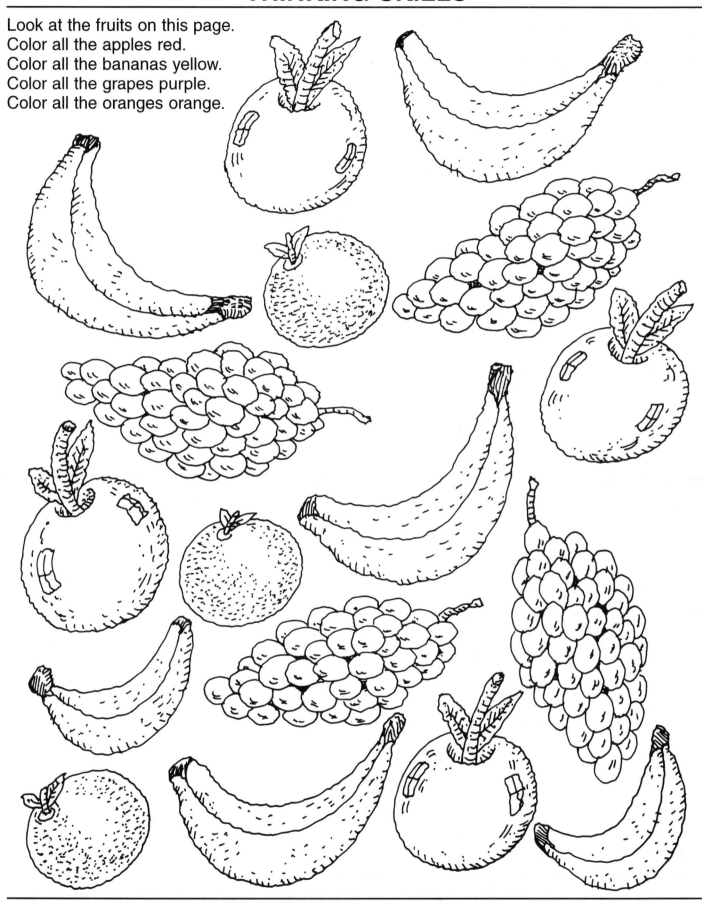

Skills: Following directions; Recognizing vocabulary; Identifying colors

THINKING SKILLS

Look at the shapes on this page.
Some of them are not complete.
Finish each shape.
Then color all the shapes.

Skills: Following directions; Recognizing shapes; Fine motor skills

THINKING SKILLS

Look at the pictures on this page.
Some of them are not complete.
Finish each picture.
Then color all the pictures.

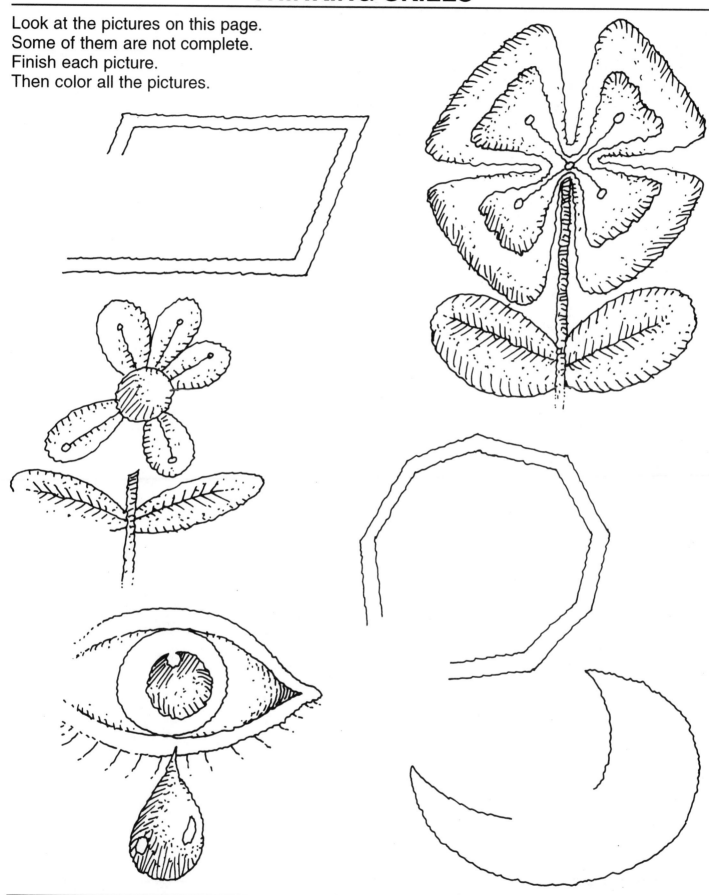

THINKING SKILLS

Look at the shapes on this page.
They are not complete.
Draw the complete shape beside the incomplete one.
Then color all the shapes.

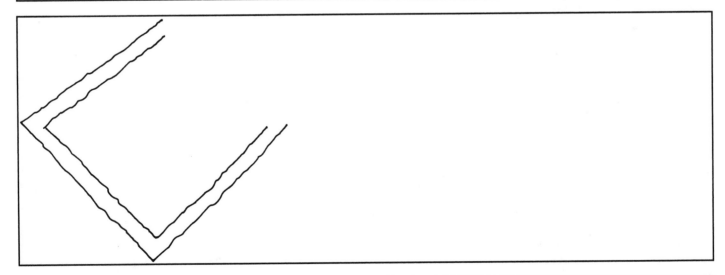

Skills: Following directions; Identifying and reproducing shapes; Fine motor skills

THINKING SKILLS

Look at the shapes on this page.
They are not complete.
Draw the complete shape beside the incomplete one.
Then color all the shapes.

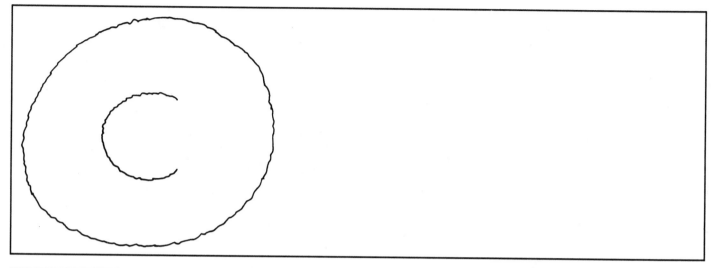

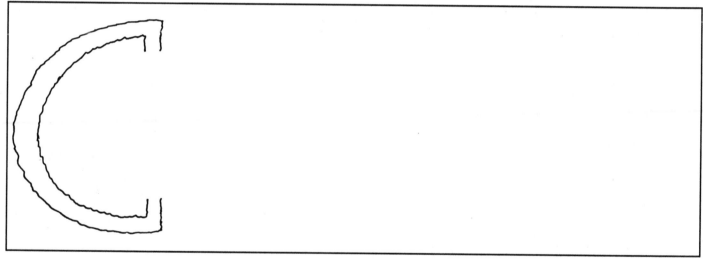

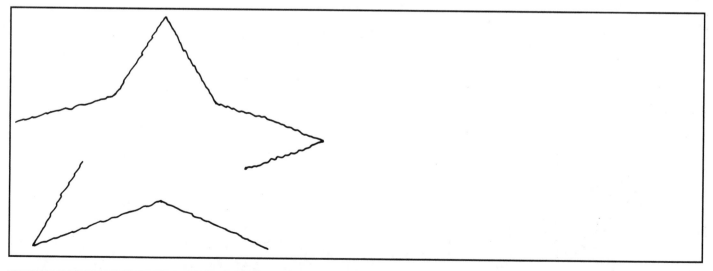

Skills: Following directions; Identifying and reproducing shapes; Fine motor skills

Look at the directions above each picture.
Follow the directions.
Then color the pictures.

Draw a  in the space.

Draw a in the space.

Draw a in the space.

Skills: Following directions; Fine motor skills

THINKING SKILLS

Look at the directions above each picture.
Follow the directions.
Then color the pictures.

Draw a ✦ in the space.

Draw a ☆ in the space.

Draw a 🐛 in the space.

Skills: Following directions; Fine motor skills

13

THINKING SKILLS

Look at the patchwork quilts on this page.
Color the squares on each quilt.
Make each quilt look different.

Skills: Following directions; Creating different patterns; Fine motor skills

THINKING SKILLS

Look at the rugs on this page.
Color the parts of each rug.
Make each rug look different.

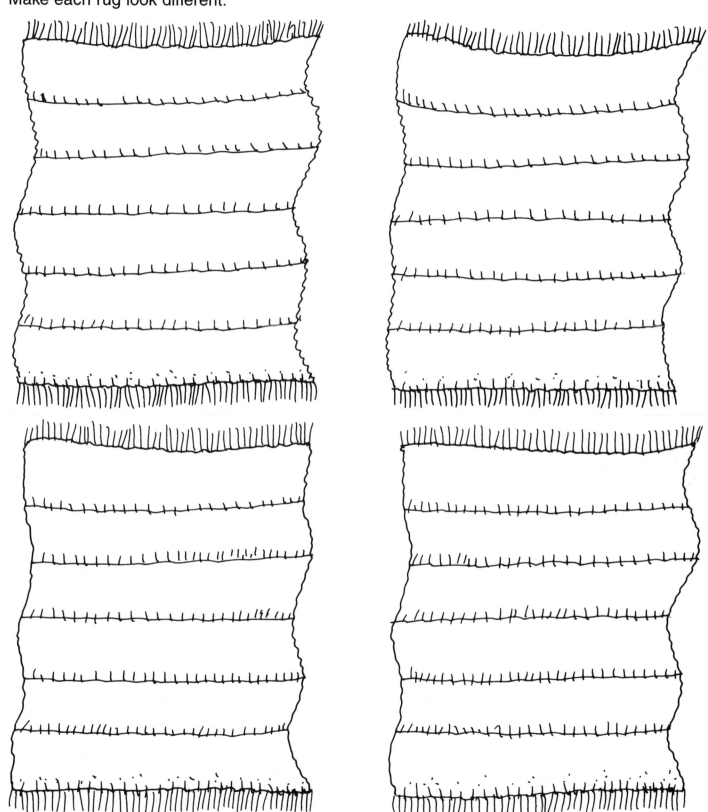

Skills: Following directions; Creating different patterns; Fine motor skills

THINKING SKILLS

Help Red Riding Hood get through the woods.
Follow the maze to Grandmother's house.
Then color the picture.

Skills: Following directions; Developing fine motor skills

THINKING SKILLS

The pirates are searching for treasure.
Follow the maze to help them find the way.
Then color the picture.

Skills: Following directions; Developing fine motor skills

THINKING SKILLS

The children are walking to school.
Follow the maze to help them find their way.
Then color the picture.

Skills: Following directions; Developing fine motor skills

THINKING SKILLS

These kittens tangled up all the yarn.
Follow the string from each kitten to the correct yarn ball.
Then color the picture.

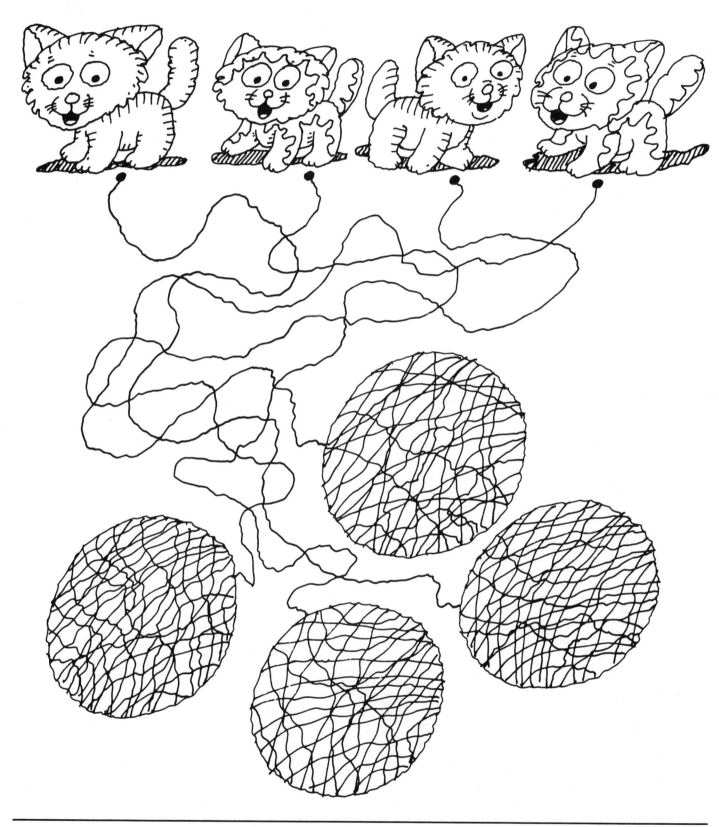

Skills: Following directions; Developing fine motor skills

THINKING SKILLS

These children want to play jump rope.
But their jump ropes got tangled up.
Follow each rope from one end to the other.
Then color the picture.

Skills: Following directions; Developing fine motor skills

THINKING SKILLS

Look at the boats at sea!
Add the following things to the picture.
Draw a bird in the sky.
Draw a boat in the water.
Draw a shell on the beach.

Skills: Following directions; Developing fine motor skills

THINKING SKILLS

The classroom is such a fun place!
Add the following things to the picture.
Draw a book on the desk.
Draw a pencil on the table.
Draw a trash can on the floor.

Skills: Following directions; Developing fine motor skills

THINKING SKILLS

What a pretty park!
Add the following things to the picture.
Draw more flowers on the ground.
Draw a kite in the air.
Draw another swing in the playground.

Skills: Following directions; Developing fine motor skills

THINKING SKILLS

Look at this picture.
Circle five things that do not belong.
Then color the picture.

Skills: Following directions; Logical reasoning

THINKING SKILLS

Look at this picture.
Circle five things that do not belong.
Then color the picture.

Skills: Following directions; Logical reasoning

THINKING SKILLS

Look at the pictures in the box at the top of the page.
Look closely at the large picture.
Circle the pictures from the box in the large picture.

Skills: Visual discrimination; Observing details

THINKING SKILLS

Look at the pictures in the box at the top of the page.
Look closely at the large picture.
Circle the pictures from the box in the large picture.

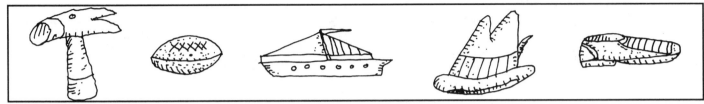

Skills: Visual discrimination; Observing details

THINKING SKILLS

Look at the pictures in each row.
One picture is different from the others.
Circle the picture that is different.
Then color the rest of the pictures.

Skills: Visual discrimination; Observing details

THINKING SKILLS

Look at the pictures in each row.
One picture is different from the others.
Circle the picture that is different.
Then color the rest of the pictures.

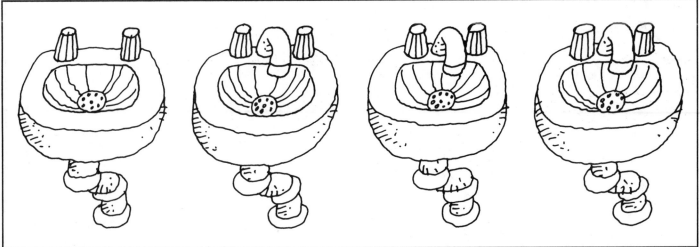

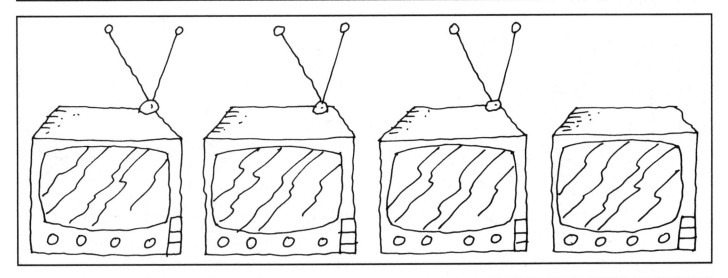

Skills: Visual discrimination; Observing details

THINKING SKILLS

Look at the shapes in each row.
One shape is different from the others.
Circle the shape that is different.
Then color the rest of the shapes.

Skills: Visual discrimination; Observing details

THINKING SKILLS

Look at the shapes in each row.
One shape is different from the others.
Circle the shape that is different.
Then color the rest of the shapes.

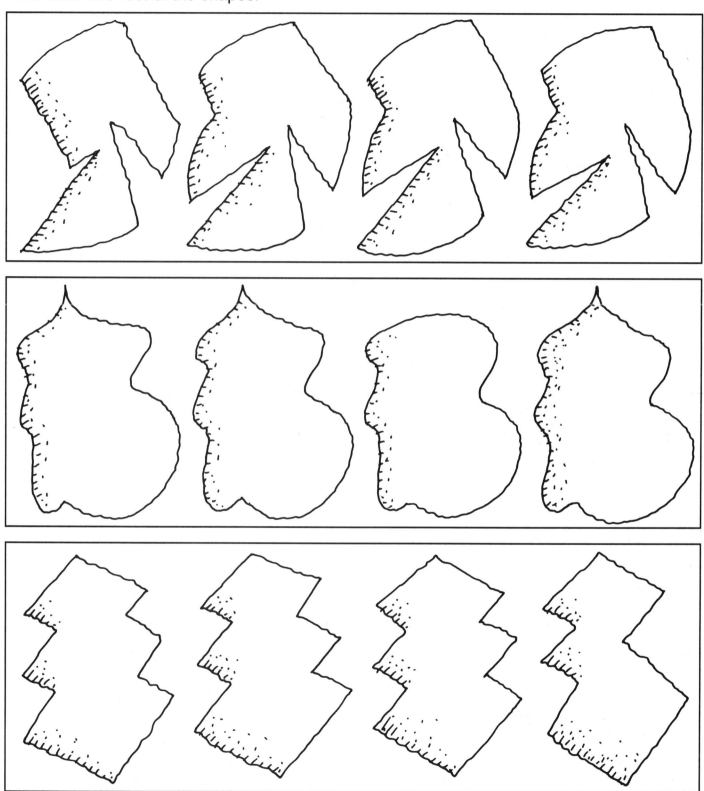

Skills: Visual discrimination; Observing details

THINKING SKILLS

Look closely at the kites on this page.
Two of the kites are exactly the same.
The rest are a little different.
Find and circle the matching kites.
Then color all of the kites.

Skills: Visual discrimination; Observing details

THINKING SKILLS

Look closely at the flowers on this page.
Two of the flowers are exactly the same.
The rest are a little different.
Find and circle the matching flowers.
Then color all of the flowers.

Skills: Visual discrimination; Observing details

THINKING SKILLS

Look at the large pictures.
Then look at the detail in each small box.
Find the detail in each large picture and circle it.
Then color the pictures.

Skills: Visual discrimination; Observing details

THINKING SKILLS

Look at the large pictures.
Then look at the detail in each small box.
Find the detail in each large picture and circle it.
Then color the pictures.

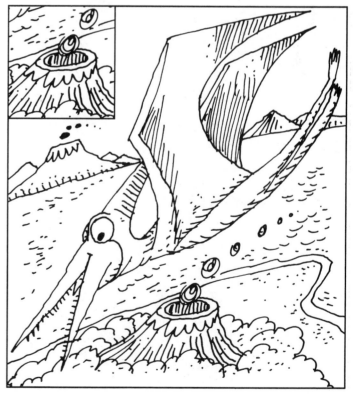

Skills: Visual discrimination; Observing details

THINKING SKILLS

Look closely at each row of pictures.
One picture in each row is in a different position.
Cross it out.
Then color the other pictures.

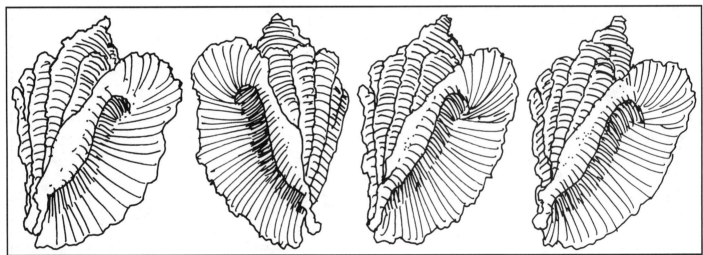

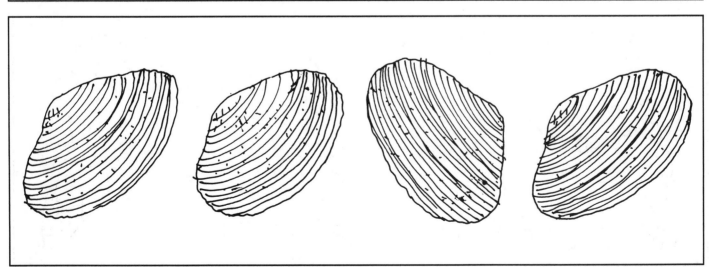

Skills: Visual discrimination; Observing details; Spatial awareness

THINKING SKILLS

Look closely at each row of pictures.
One picture in each row is in a different position.
Cross it out.
Then color the other pictures.

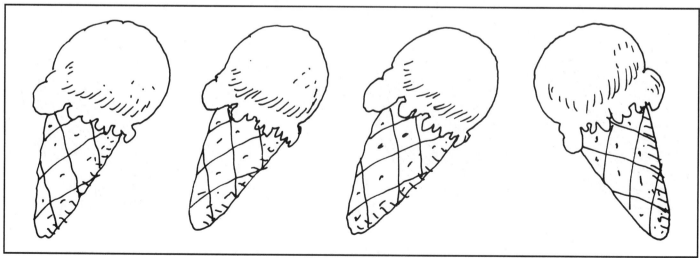

Skills: Visual discrimination; Observing details; Spatial awareness

THINKING SKILLS

Look at the waiter at the top of the page.
He is holding a tray in his **right** hand.
He is holding a pitcher in his **left** hand.
Look at the waiters on the bottom of the page.
Color the waiters holding something in their right hand blue.
Color the waiters holding something in their left hand red.

Skills: Visual discrimination; Recognizing right and left; Word recognition

THINKING SKILLS

Look at the clown at the top of the page.
He is holding a lollipop in his **right** hand.
He is holding balloons in his **left** hand.
Look at the clowns on the bottom of the page.
Color the clowns holding something in their right hand blue.
Color the clowns holding something in their left hand red.

Skills: Visual discrimination; Recognizing right and left; Word recognition

THINKING SKILLS

Look at the dinosaurs.
Then look closely at the shadows.
Draw a line to connect each dinosaur to the correct shadow.

Skills: Visual discrimination; Recognizing similarities

THINKING SKILLS

Look at the sea creatures.
Then look closely at their shadows.
Draw a line to connect each sea creature to the correct shadow.

Skills: Visual discrimination; Recognizing similarities

THINKING SKILLS

Look at the picture at the top of this page.
Then look at the three parts below.
Draw a line to show where each part belongs in the picture.

Skills: Visual discrimination; Spatial awareness

THINKING SKILLS

We've been unpacking.
Look carefully at the clothes below.
When you are ready, turn the page to play a memory game.

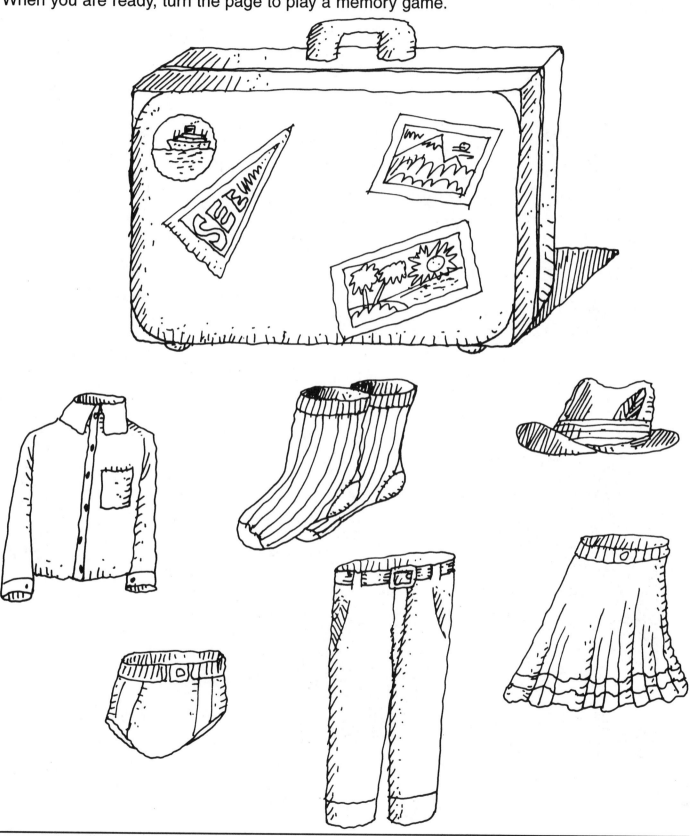

Skills: Visual discrimination; Visual memory

THINKING SKILLS

Look at the pictures on this page.
Which ones do you remember from the page before?
Circle the ones you remember.

Skills: Visual discrimination; Visual memory

THINKING SKILLS

Look at the picture at the top of this page.
Then look at the three parts below.
Draw a line to show where each part belongs in the picture.

Skills: Visual discrimination; Spatial awareness

COMPARING AND CLASSIFYING

Look at the pictures in each box.
Draw a circle around the picture that is **larger**.
Then color the pictures.

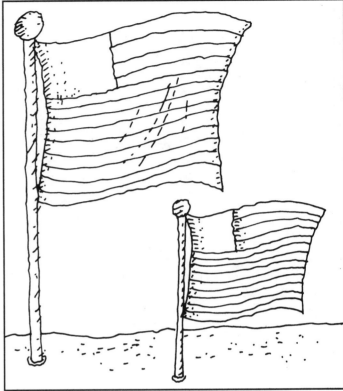

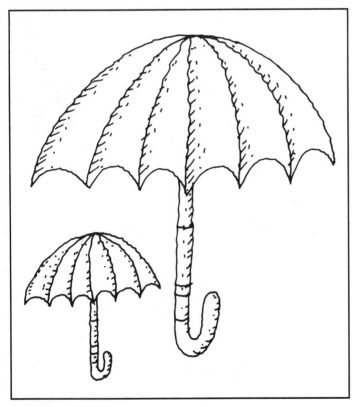

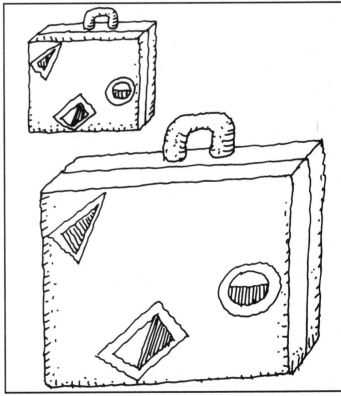

Skills: Visual discrimination; Making comparisons

COMPARING AND CLASSIFYING

Look at the pictures in each box.
Draw a circle around the picture that is **larger**.
Then color the pictures.

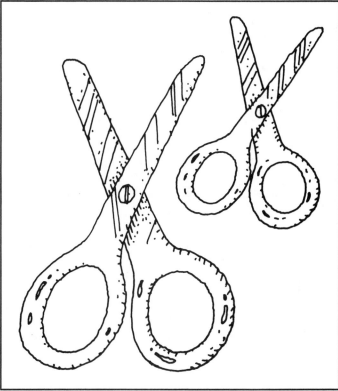

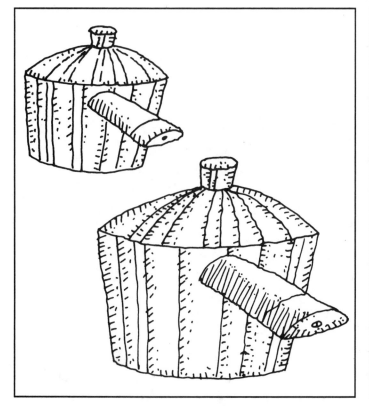

Skills: Visual discrimination; Making comparisons

COMPARING AND CLASSIFYING

Look at the pictures in each box.
Draw a circle around the picture that is **larger**.
Then color the pictures.

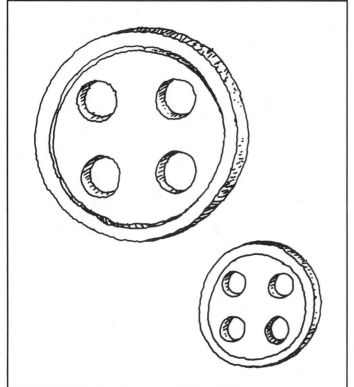

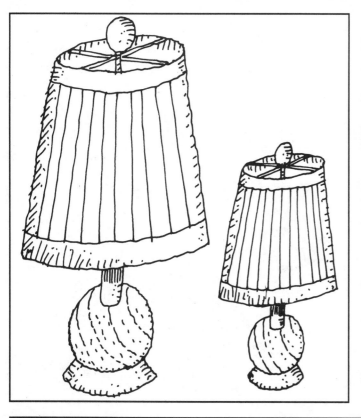

Skills: Visual discrimination; Making comparisons

COMPARING AND CLASSIFYING

Look at the pictures in each box.
Draw a circle around the picture that is **smaller**.
Then color the pictures.

Skills: Visual discrimination; Making comparisons

COMPARING AND CLASSIFYING

Look at the pictures in each box.
Draw a circle around the picture that is **smaller**.
Then color the pictures.

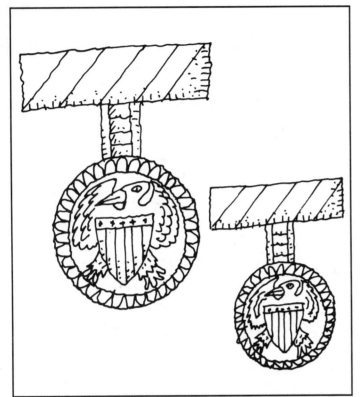

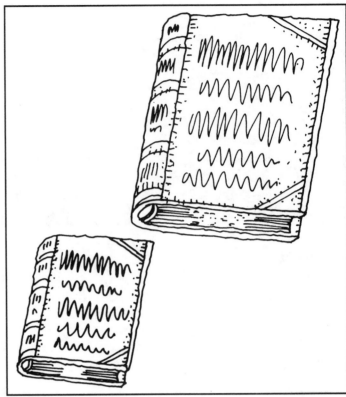

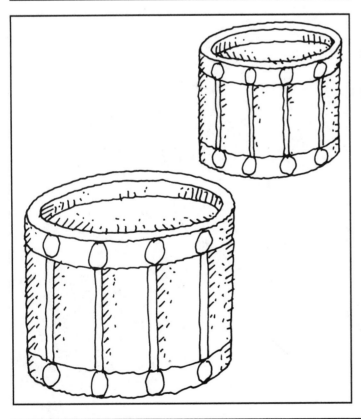

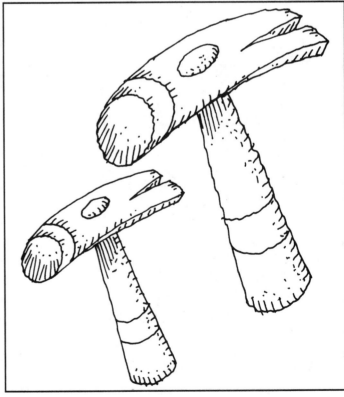

Skills: Visual discrimination; Making comparisons

COMPARING AND CLASSIFYING

Look at the pictures in each box.
Draw a circle around the picture that is **smaller**.
Then color the pictures.

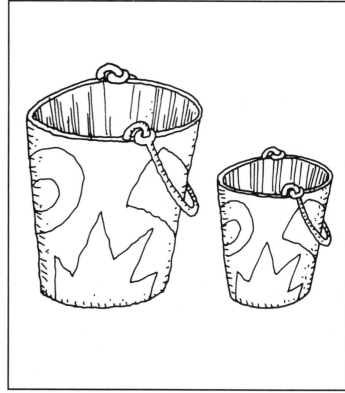
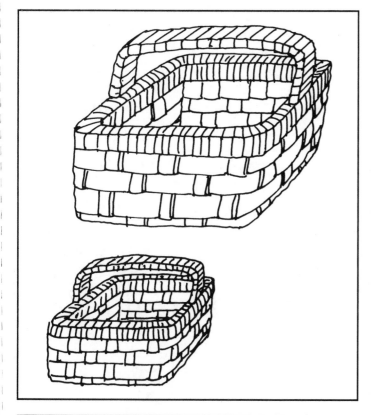
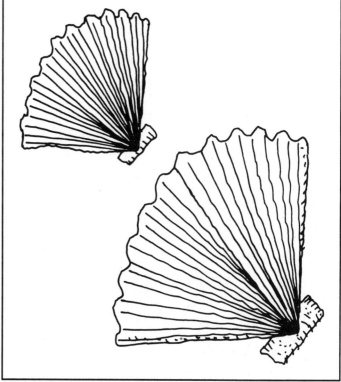

Skills: Visual discrimination; Making comparisons

COMPARING AND CLASSIFYING

Look at the pair of pictures on the left.
Think about how they are related.
Then look at the pictures on the right.
Circle the two that are related in the same way.

Skills: Identifying relationships; Logical reasoning

COMPARING AND CLASSIFYING

Look at the pair of pictures on the left.
Think about how they are related.
Then look at the pictures on the right.
Circle the two that are related in the same way.

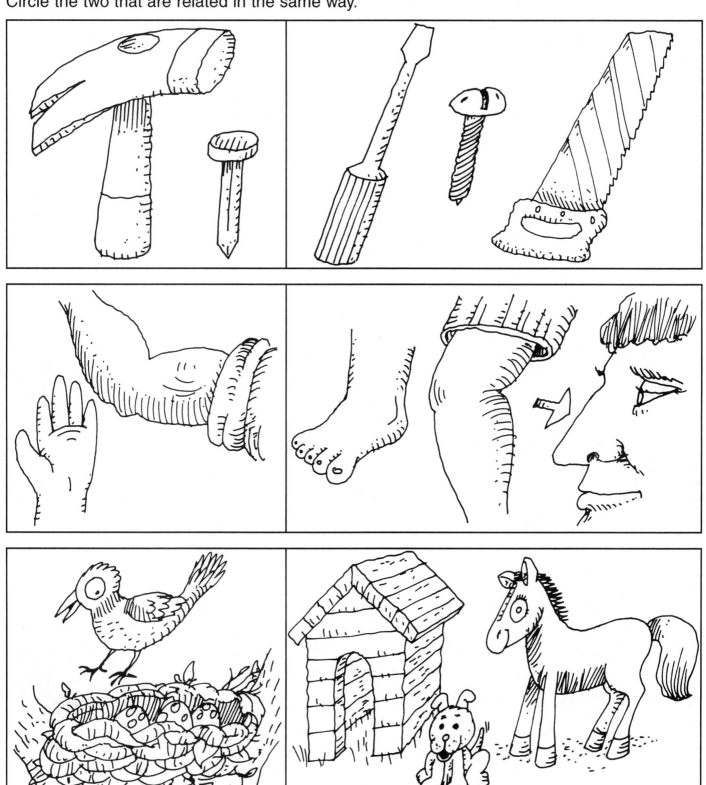

Skills: Identifying relationships; Logical reasoning

COMPARING AND CLASSIFYING

Look at the pair of pictures on the left.
Think about how they are related.
Then look at the pictures on the right.
Circle the two that are related in the same way.

Skills: Identifying relationships; Logical reasoning

COMPARING AND CLASSIFYING

Look at the pair of pictures on the left.
Think about how they are related.
Then look at the pictures on the right.
Circle the two that are related in the same way.

Skills: Identifying relationships; Logical reasoning

COMPARING AND CLASSIFYING

Look at the pair of pictures on the left.
Think about how they are related.
Then look at the pictures on the right.
Circle the two that are related in the same way.

Skills: Identifying relationships; Logical reasoning

COMPARING AND CLASSIFYING

Look at the pictures in each box.
Think about how fast each moves.
Circle the one that moves **faster**.
Then color the pictures.

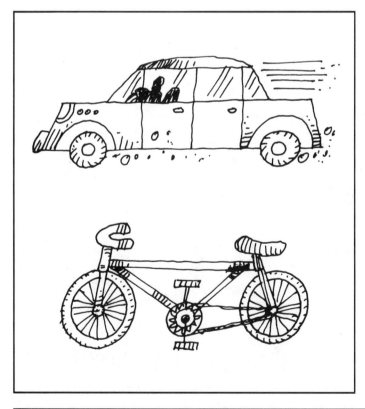

Skills: Comparing; Logical reasoning

COMPARING AND CLASSIFYING

Look at the pictures in each box.
Think about how heavy each is.
Circle the one that is **heavier**.
Then color the pictures.

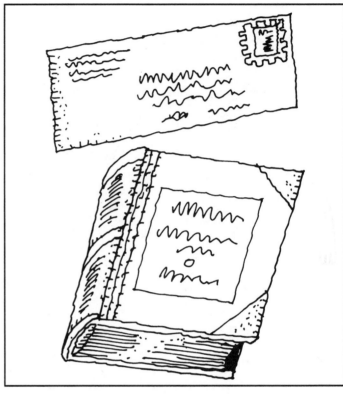

Skills: Comparing; Logical reasoning

COMPARING AND CLASSIFYING

Look at the pictures in each box.
Think about which is real and which is make-believe.
Circle the one that is **real**.
Then color the pictures.

Skills: Comparing; Logical reasoning

COMPARING AND CLASSIFYING

Look at the pictures in each box.
Think about how each one sounds.
Circle the one that is **louder**.
Then color the pictures.

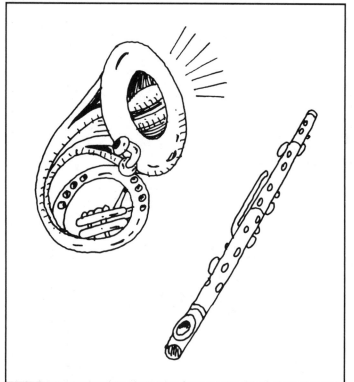

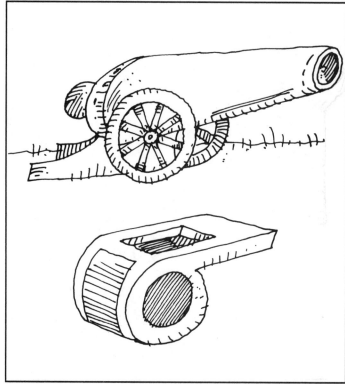

Skills: Comparing; Logical reasoning

COMPARING AND CLASSIFYING

Look at the pictures in each box.
Think about how each one feels.
Circle the one that is **softer**.
Then color the pictures.

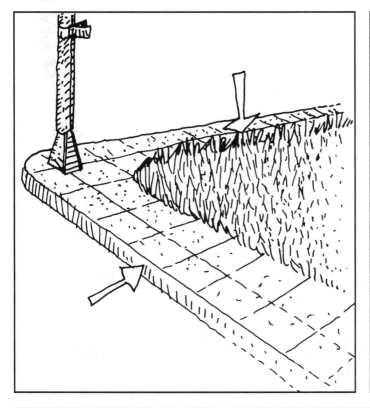

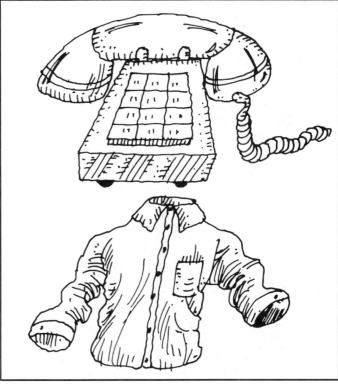

Skills: Comparing; Logical reasoning

COMPARING AND CLASSIFYING

Look at the pictures on the left.
Look at the pictures on the right.
Think about what is missing from each picture on the left.
Draw a line to match each picture to the part that is missing.
Then color the pictures.

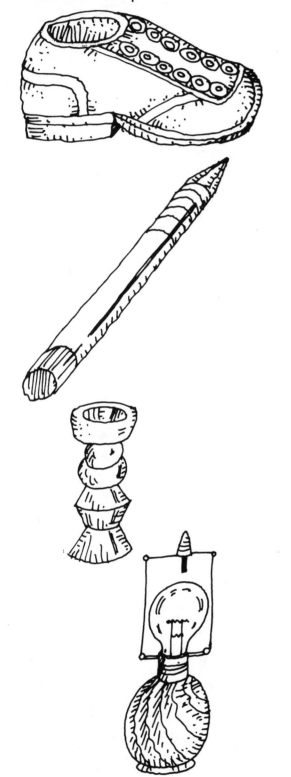
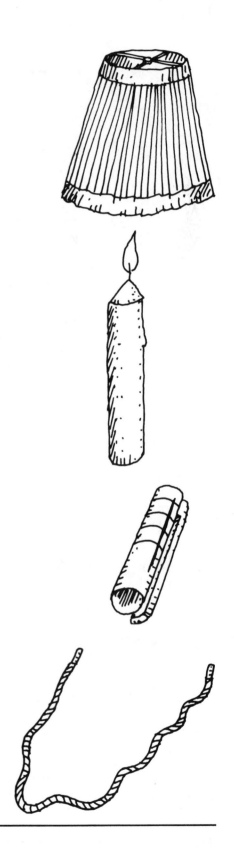

Skills: Logical reasoning; Identifying parts of a whole

COMPARING AND CLASSIFYING

Look at the pictures on the left.
Look at the pictures on the right.
Think about what is missing from each picture on the left.
Draw a line to match each picture to the part that is missing.
Then color the pictures.

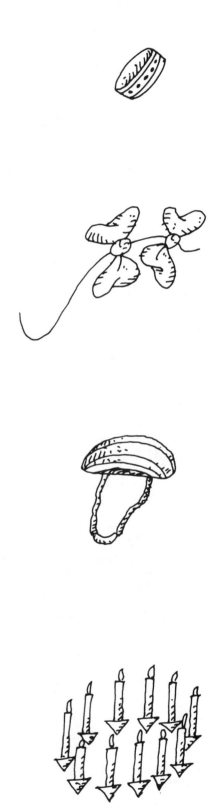

Skills: Logical reasoning; Identifying parts of a whole

COMPARING AND CLASSIFYING

Look at the pictures on the left.
Look at the pictures on the right.
Think about what is missing from each picture on the left.
Draw a line to match each picture to the part that is missing.
Then color the pictures.

Skills: Logical reasoning; Identifying parts of a whole

COMPARING AND CLASSIFYING

Look at the pictures on the left.
Look at the pictures on the right.
Think about what is missing from each picture on the left.
Draw a line to match each picture to the part that is missing.
Then color the pictures.

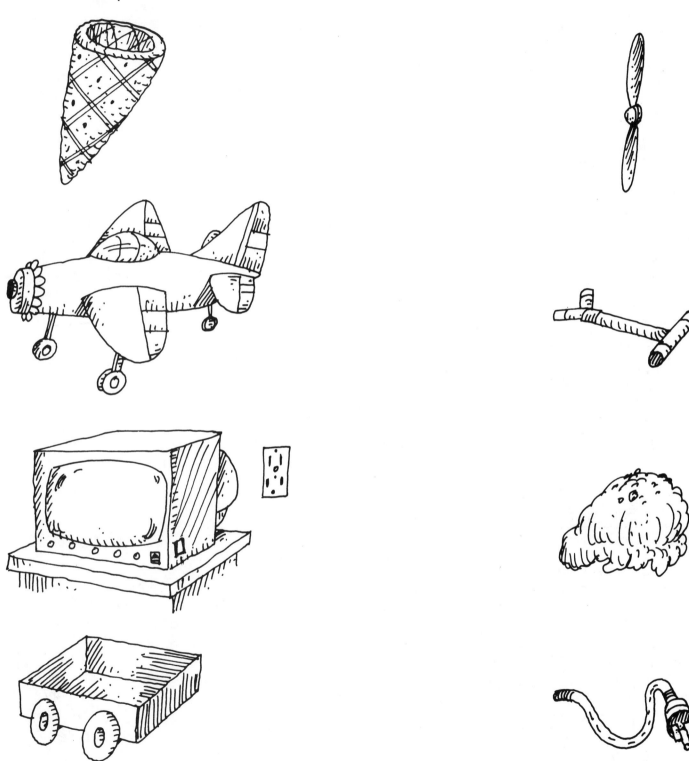

Skills: Logical reasoning; Identifying parts of a whole

COMPARING AND CLASSIFYING

Look at the pictures on the left.
Look at the pictures on the right.
Think about what is missing from each picture on the left.
Draw a line to match each picture to the part that is missing.
Then color the pictures.

Skills: Logical reasoning; Identifying parts of a whole

COMPARING AND CLASSIFYING

Which ones do you wear on your head?
Look at each picture.
Color the pictures of things that go on your head.

Skills: Classification; Logical reasoning

COMPARING AND CLASSIFYING

Which ones do you wear on your feet?
Look at each picture.
Color the pictures of things that go on your feet.

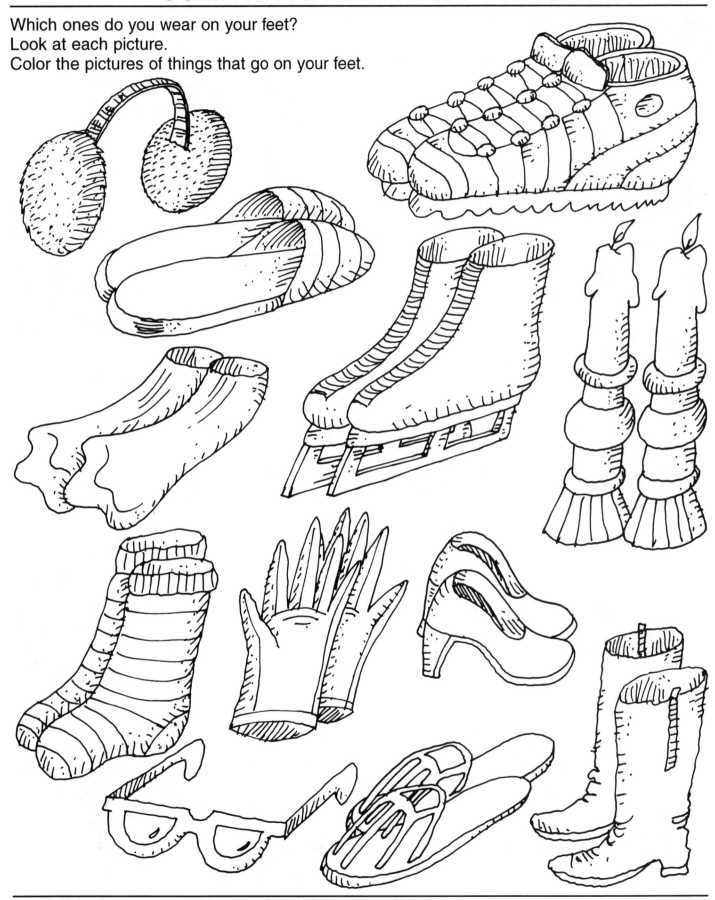

Skills: Classification; Logical reasoning

COMPARING AND CLASSIFYING

Which ones do you use in the bath?
Look at each picture.
Color the pictures of things that you use in the bath.

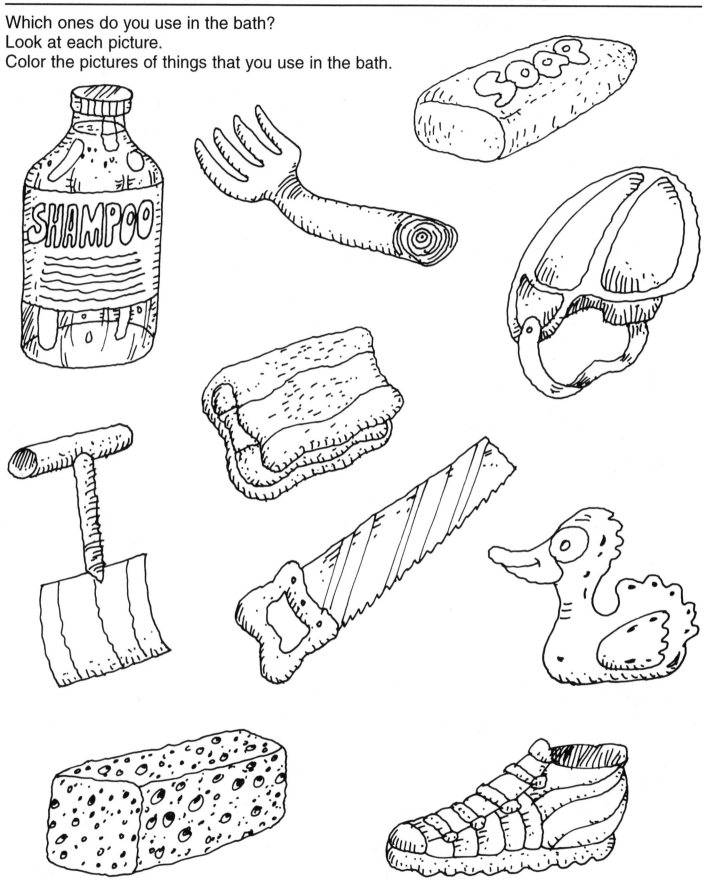

Skills: Classification; Logical reasoning

COMPARING AND CLASSIFYING

Which ones make music?
Look at each picture.
Color the pictures of things that are used to make music.

Skills: Classification; Logical reasoning

COMPARING AND CLASSIFYING

Which ones would you see at a birthday party?
Look at each picture.
Color the pictures of things that you would see at a birthday party.

Skills: Classification; Logical reasoning

COMPARING AND CLASSIFYING

Look at the pictures in each box.
Put an **X** on the picture in each box that does not go with the others.
Then color the other pictures.

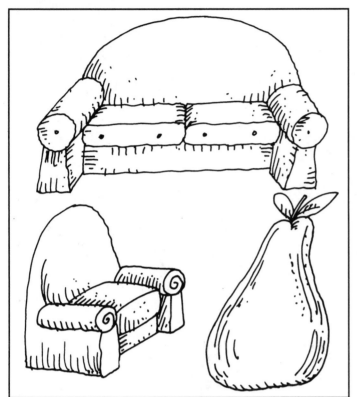

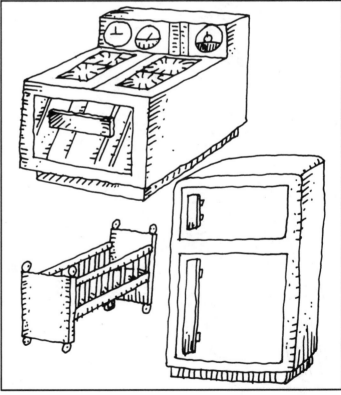

Skills: Association; Classification; Logical reasoning

COMPARING AND CLASSIFYING

Look at the pictures in each box.
Put an **X** on the picture in each box that does not go with the others.
Then color the other pictures.

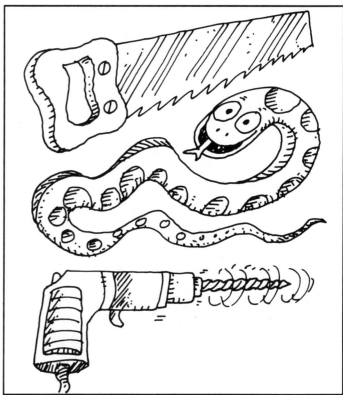

Skills: Association; Classification; Logical reasoning

COMPARING AND CLASSIFYING

Look at the pictures in each box.
Put an **X** on the picture in each box that does not go with the others.
Then color the other pictures.

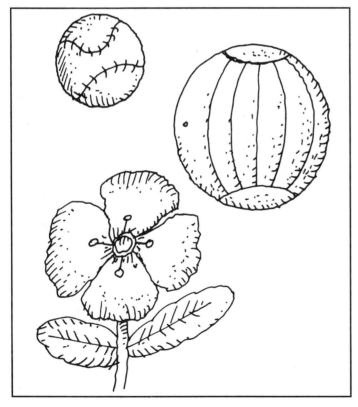

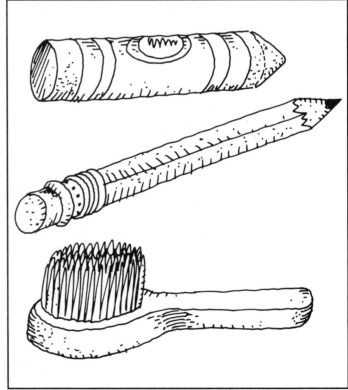

Skills: Association; Classification; Logical reasoning

COMPARING AND CLASSIFYING

The dishes need to be put away.
Help sort them into groups.
Draw a line between the matching dishes.
Then color the pictures.

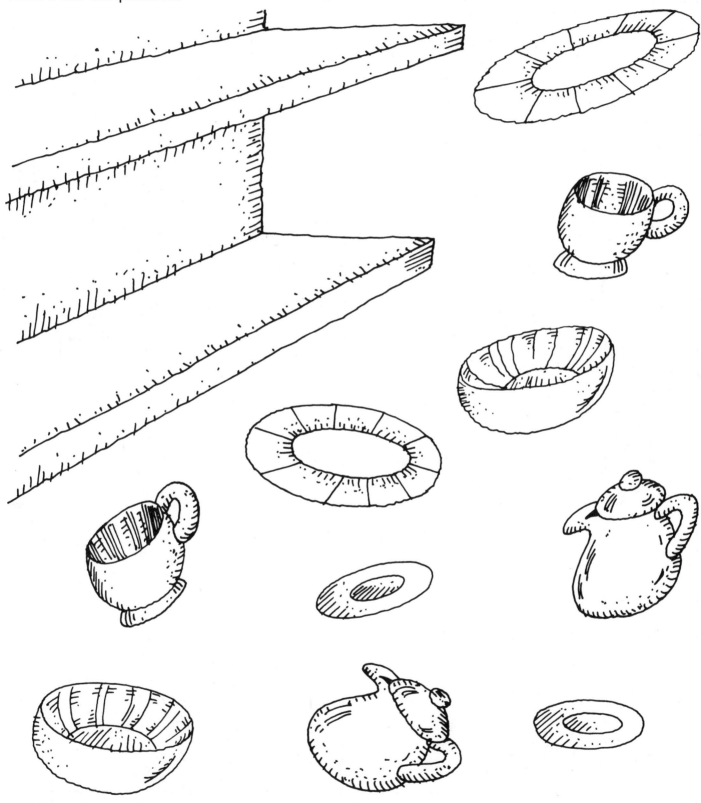

Skills: Recognizing pairs; Classification; Visual matching

COMPARING AND CLASSIFYING

The hall closet needs to be cleaned.
Help sort the balls into groups.
Draw a line between the matching balls.
Then color the pictures.

Skills: Recognizing pairs; Classification; Visual matching

COMPARING AND CLASSIFYING

Look at the pictures in each row.
Color the pictures in each row that belong together.

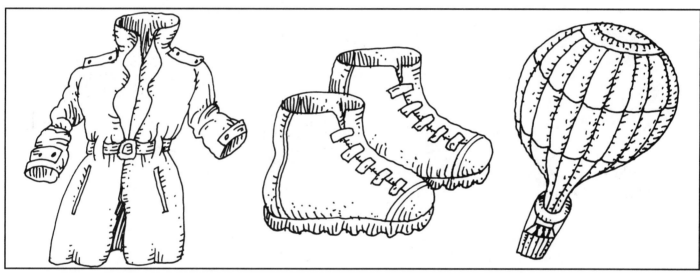

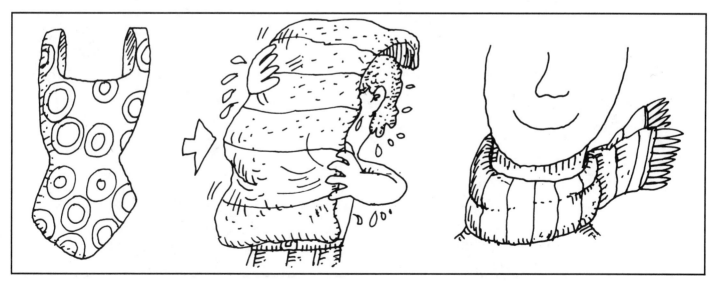

Skills: Association; Classification; Logical reasoning

COMPARING AND CLASSIFYING

Look at the pictures in each row.
Color the pictures in each row that belong together.

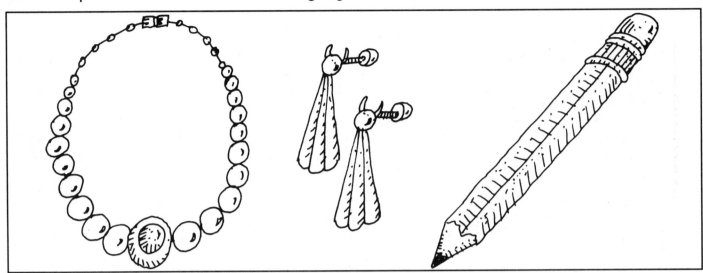

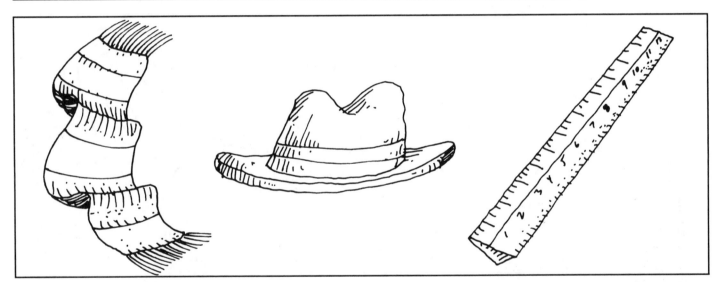

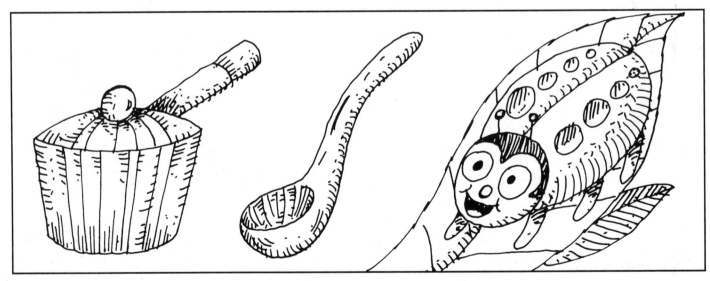

Skills: Association; Classification; Logical reasoning

COMPARING AND CLASSIFYING

Look at the words in each leaf.
Circle the words that go together.

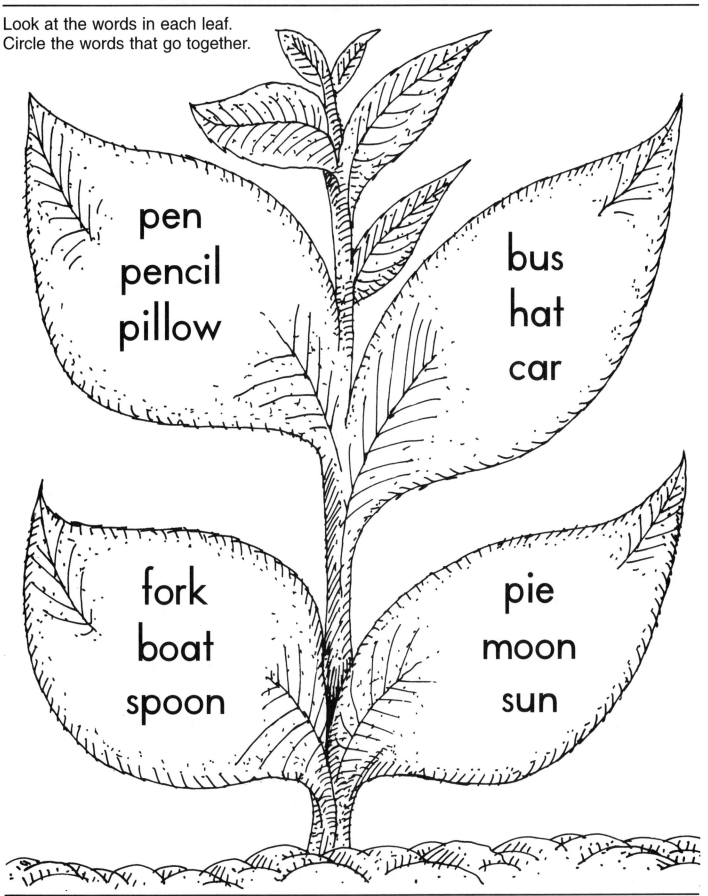

pen
pencil
pillow

bus
hat
car

fork
boat
spoon

pie
moon
sun

Skills: Association; Classification; Logical reasoning; Vocabulary recognition

COMPARING AND CLASSIFYING

Look at the words in each pail.
Circle the words that go together.

cat
dog
box

dog
pail
shovel

flute
saw
hammer

bird
star
nest

Skills: Association; Classification; Logical reasoning; Vocabulary recognition

COMPARING AND CLASSIFYING

Look at the words in each boat.
Circle the words that go together.

bow
rope
arrow

leaf
mitten
hat

car
truck
vest

cow
cupcake
cookie

Skills: Association; Classification; Logical reasoning; Vocabulary recognition

COMPARING AND CLASSIFYING

Look at the words in each treasure chest.
Circle the words that go together.

flower
broom
mop

key
lock
book

button
leaf
flower

bread
shirt
butter

Skills: Association; Classification; Logical reasoning; Vocabulary recognition

COMPARING AND CLASSIFYING

Look at the words in the box at the top of the page.
Look at the pictures in each box.
Then write a word from the box that tells why those pictures go together.

games	clothes	tools	fruit

_____

_____

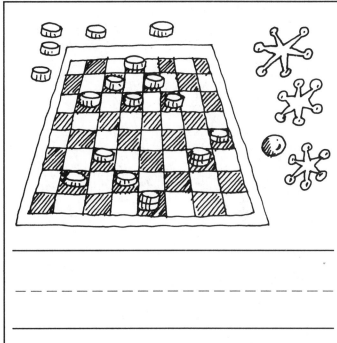

_____

_____

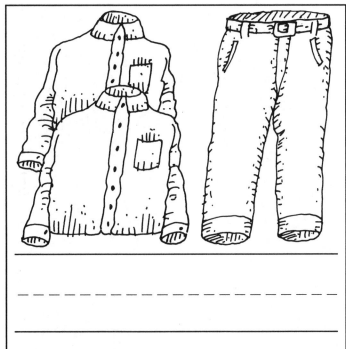

_____

_____

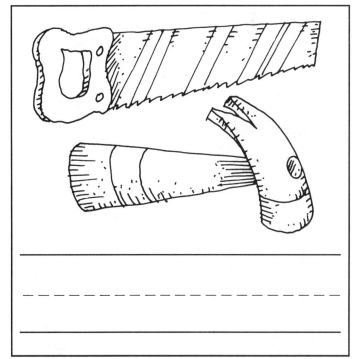

_____

_____

Skills: Association; Classification; Logical reasoning; Handwriting

COMPARING AND CLASSIFYING

Look at the words in the box at the top of the page.
Look at the pictures in each box.
Then write a word from the box that tells why those pictures go together.

| toys | birds | hats | shoes |

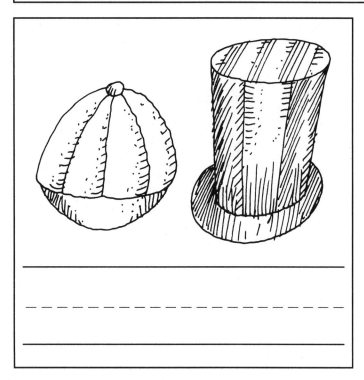

Skills: Association; Classification; Logical reasoning; Handwriting

COMPARING AND CLASSIFYING

Look at the words in the box at the top of the page.
Look at the pictures in each box.
Then write a word from the box that tells why those pictures go together.

| numbers | candy | dishes | animals |

_____

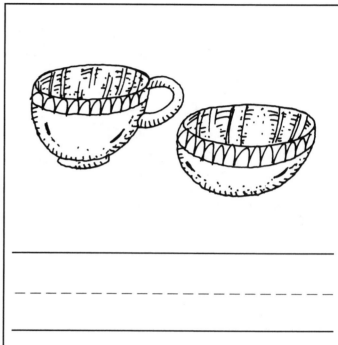

_____

_____

_____

Skills: Association; Classification; Logical reasoning; Handwriting

COMPARING AND CLASSIFYING

Look at the words in the box at the top of the page.
Look at the pictures in each box.
Then write a word from the box that tells why those pictures go together.

jewelry	pets	drinks	bugs

_____

_____

_____

_____

_____

_____

_____

_____

_____

_____

_____

_____

Skills: Association; Classification; Logical reasoning; Handwriting

OPPOSITES

Look at the pictures.
Draw a line between the pictures that show opposites.

Skills: Developing vocabulary; Identifying opposites; Matching

OPPOSITES

Look at the pictures.
Draw a line between the pictures that show opposites.

Skills: Developing vocabulary; Identifying opposites; Matching

OPPOSITES

Look at the pictures.
Draw a line between the pictures that show opposites.

Skills: Developing vocabulary; Identifying opposites; Matching

OPPOSITES

Look at the pictures.
Draw a line between the pictures that show opposites.

Skills: Developing vocabulary; Identifying opposites; Matching

OPPOSITES

Look at the pictures.
Draw a line between the pictures that show opposites.

Skills: Developing vocabulary; Identifying opposites; Matching

OPPOSITES

Look at the picture and word in each box.
Look at the words at the top of the page.
Write the word that is the opposite of the picture in the box.
Then draw a picture to show that word.

stand	cold	awake

hot

_____
- - - - - - - - - - -
_____

asleep

_____
- - - - - - - - - - -
_____

sit

_____
- - - - - - - - - - -
_____

Skills: Vocabulary development; Identifying opposites; Fine motor skill development

OPPOSITES

Look at the picture and word in each box.
Look at the words at the top of the page.
Write the word that is the opposite of the picture in the box.
Then draw a picture to show that word.

closed	deep	short

open

---

long

---

shallow

Skills: Vocabulary development; Identifying opposites; Fine motor skill development

OPPOSITES

Look at the picture and word in each box.
Look at the words at the top of the page.
Write the word that is the opposite of the picture in the box.
Then draw a picture to show that word.

poor	few	happy

sad

rich

many

Skills: Vocabulary development; Identifying opposites; Fine motor skill development

OPPOSITES

Look at the picture and word in each box.
Look at the words at the top of the page.
Write the word that is the opposite of the picture in the box.
Then draw a picture to show that word.

clean	straight	empty

full

dirty

crooked

Skills: Vocabulary development; Identifying opposites; Fine motor skill development

OPPOSITES

Look at the picture and word in each box.
Look at the words at the top of the page.
Write the word that is the opposite of the picture in the box.
Then draw a picture to show that word.

down	front	under

up

over

back

Skills: Vocabulary development; Identifying opposites; Fine motor skill development

OPPOSITES

Look at the words on each tree.
Circle the words on each tree that are opposites.

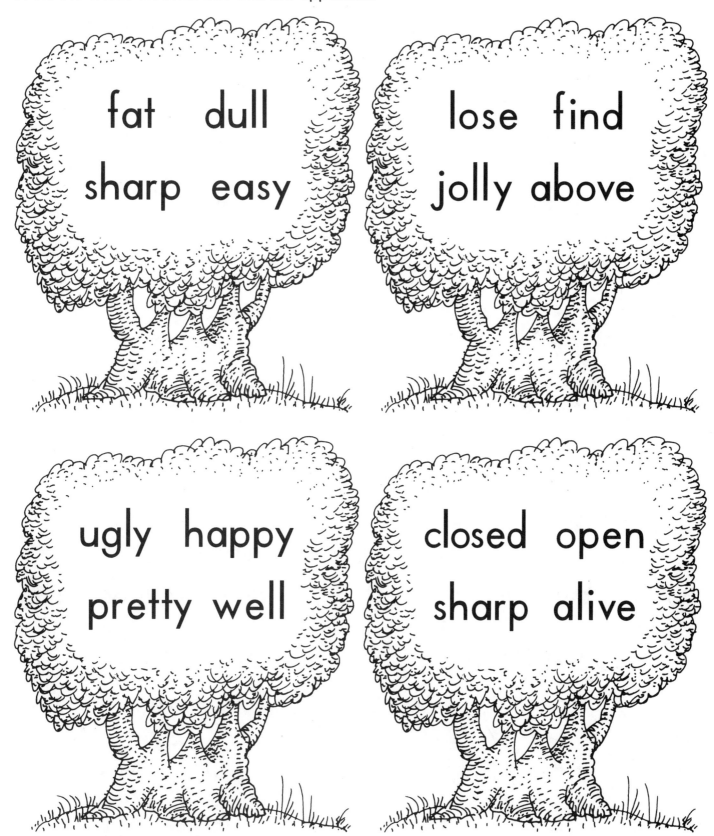

fat   dull

sharp   easy

lose   find

jolly   above

ugly   happy

pretty   well

closed   open

sharp   alive

Skills: Identifying opposites; Vocabulary development; Recognizing opposites in a group of words

OPPOSITES

Look at the words on each bunch of grapes.
Circle the words on each bunch of grapes that are opposites.

big brave
little up

hard hot
easy smart

stop go
light full

over new
soft under

Skills: Identifying opposites; Vocabulary development; Recognizing opposites in a group of words

OPPOSITES

Look at the words on each truck.
Circle the words on each truck that are opposites.

loose far
warm tight

fancy plain
cold loud

loud straight
quiet after

sick off
kind on

Skills: Identifying opposites; Vocabulary development; Recognizing opposites in a group of words

OPPOSITES

Look at the words on each blimp.
Circle the words on each blimp that are opposites.

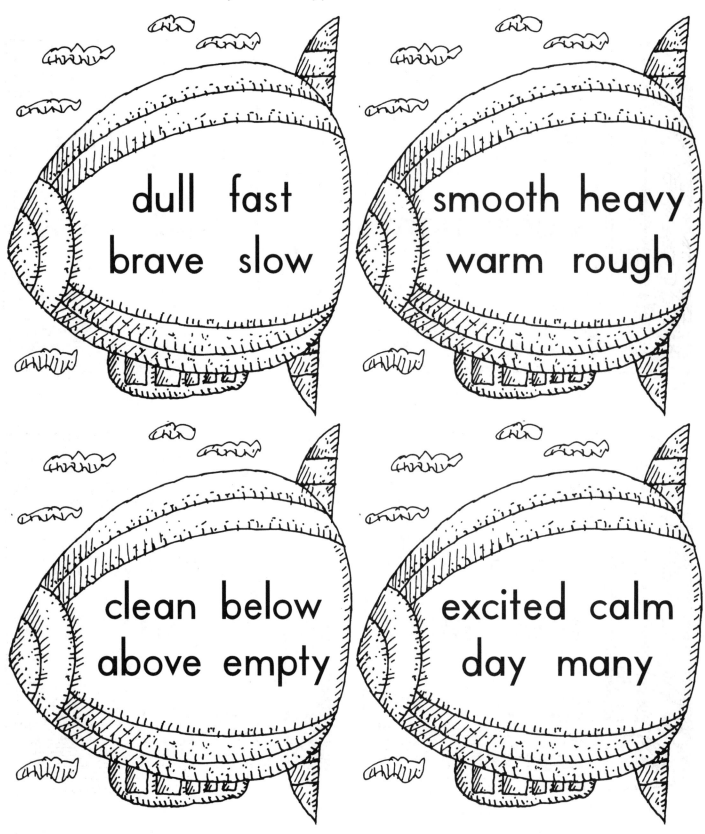

dull fast
brave slow

smooth heavy
warm rough

clean below
above empty

excited calm
day many

Skills: Identifying opposites; Vocabulary development; Recognizing opposites in a group of words

OPPOSITES

Look at the words on each book.
Circle the words on each book that are opposites.

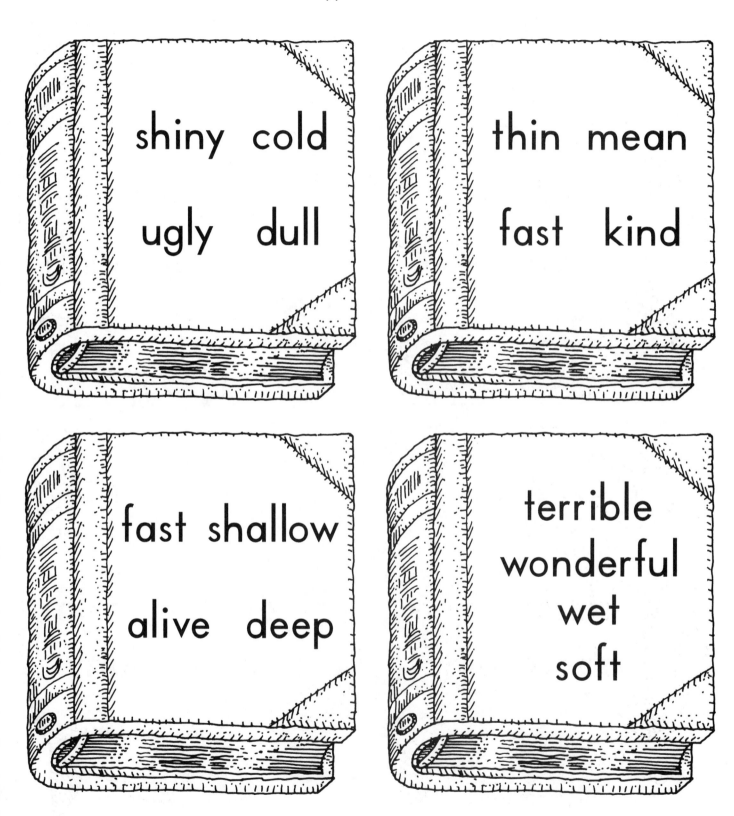

shiny cold

ugly dull

thin mean

fast kind

fast shallow

alive deep

terrible
wonderful
wet
soft

Skills: Identifying opposites; Vocabulary development; Recognizing opposites in a group of words

OPPOSITES

Look at the picture and word in each section of the wheel.
Color each pair of opposites the same color.

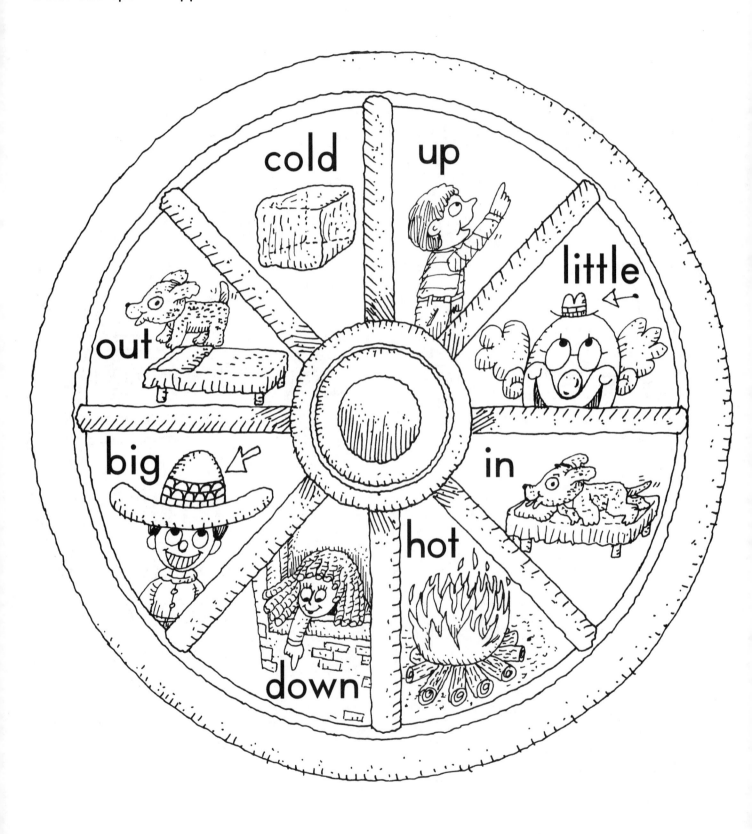

Skills: Identifying pairs of opposites; Vocabulary development

OPPOSITES

Look at the picture and word in each section of the wheel.
Color each pair of opposites the same color.

Skills: Identifying pairs of opposites; Vocabulary development

OPPOSITES

Look at the picture and word in each section of the wheel.
Color each pair of opposites the same color.

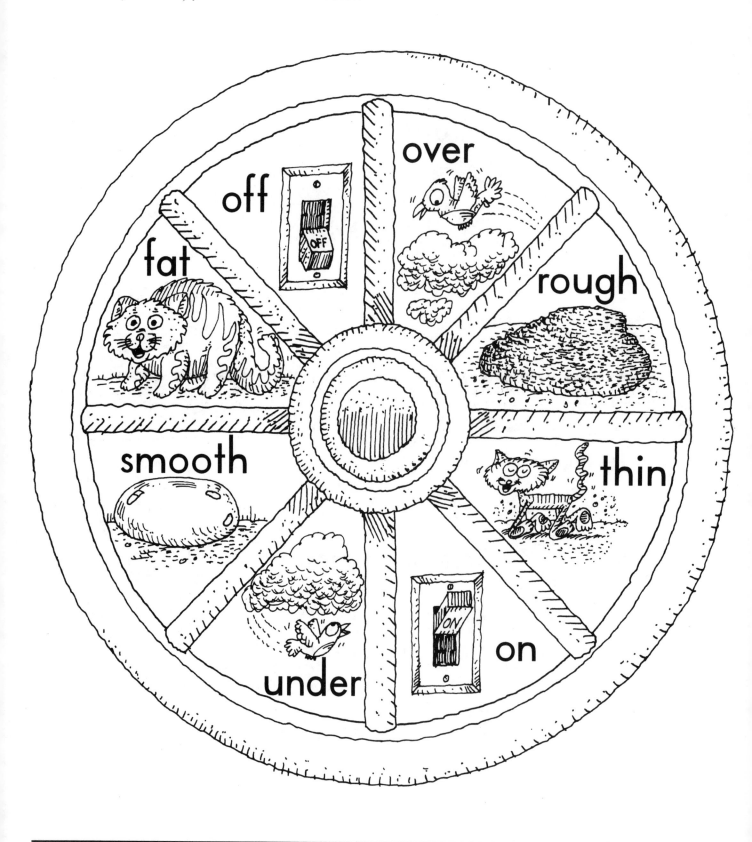

Skills: Identifying pairs of opposites; Vocabulary development

OPPOSITES

Look at the picture and word in each section of the wheel.
Color each pair of opposites the same color.

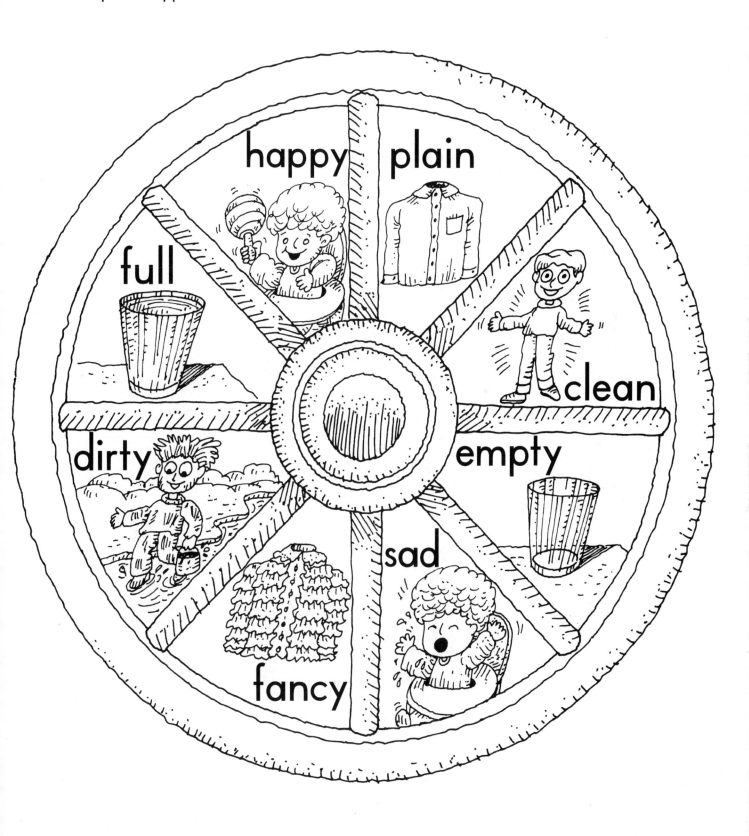

Skills: Identifying pairs of opposites; Vocabulary development

OPPOSITES

Look at the picture and word in each section of the wheel.
Color each pair of opposites the same color.

Skills: Identifying pairs of opposites; Vocabulary development

STORY ORDER

Look at the pictures.
Write a **1** in the picture that shows what happened first.
Write a **2** in the picture that shows what happened second.
Write a **3** in the picture that shows what happened third.
Then color the pictures.

Skills: Sequencing; Story order; Writing numerals

STORY ORDER

Look at the pictures.
Write a **1** in the picture that shows what happened first.
Write a **2** in the picture that shows what happened second.
Write a **3** in the picture that shows what happened third.
Then color the pictures.

Skills: Sequencing; Story order; Writing numerals

STORY ORDER

Look at the pictures.
Write a **1** in the picture that shows what happened first.
Write a **2** in the picture that shows what happened second.
Write a **3** in the picture that shows what happened third.
Then color the pictures.

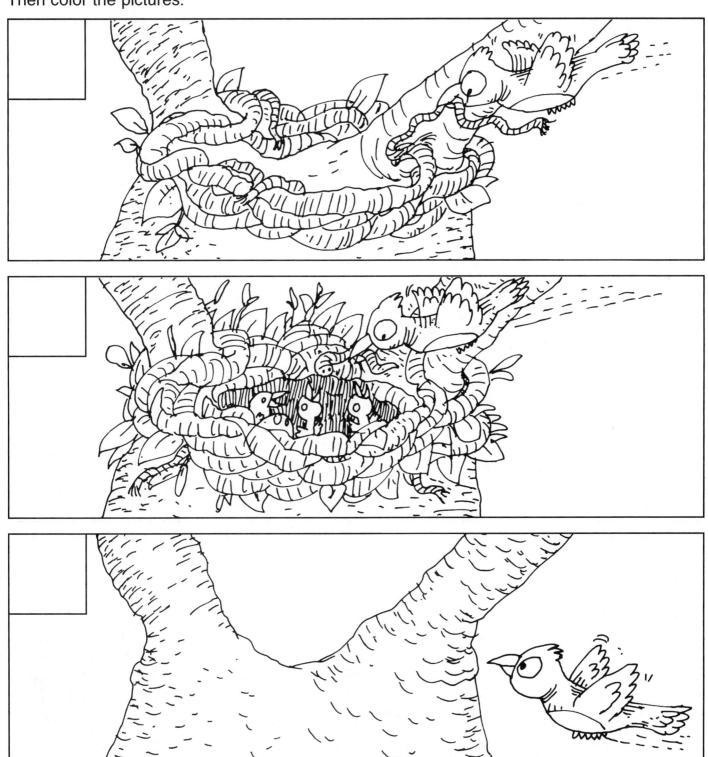

Skills: Sequencing; Story order; Writing numerals

STORY ORDER

Look at the pictures.
Write a **1** in the picture that shows what happened first.
Write a **2** in the picture that shows what happened second.
Write a **3** in the picture that shows what happened third.
Then color the pictures.

Skills: Sequencing; Story order; Writing numerals

STORY ORDER

Look at the pictures.
Write a **1** in the picture that shows what happened first.
Write a **2** in the picture that shows what happened second.
Write a **3** in the picture that shows what happened third.
Then color the pictures.

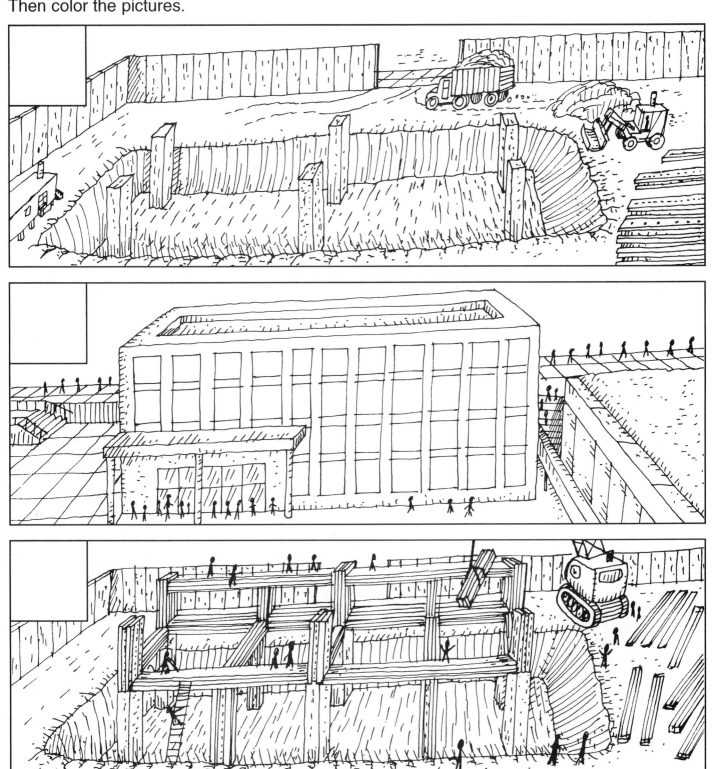

Skills: Sequencing; Story order; Writing numerals

STORY ORDER

Look at the pictures in each row.
Think about the story they tell.
Draw a circle around the small picture that shows what comes next.
Then color the pictures.

Skills: Logical reasoning; Sequencing; Identifying parts of a story

STORY ORDER

Look at the pictures in each row.
Think about the story they tell.
Draw a circle around the small picture that shows what comes next.
Then color the pictures.

Skills: Logical reasoning; Sequencing; Identifying parts of a story

STORY ORDER

Look at the pictures in each row.
Think about the story they tell.
Draw a circle around the small picture that shows what comes next.
Then color the pictures.

Skills: Logical reasoning; Sequencing; Identifying parts of a story

STORY ORDER

Look at the pictures in each row.
Think about the story they tell.
Draw a circle around the small picture that shows what comes next.
Then color the pictures.

Skills: Logical reasoning; Sequencing; Identifying parts of a story

STORY ORDER

Look at the pictures in each row.
Think about the story they tell.
Draw a circle around the small picture that shows what comes next.
Then color the pictures.

Skills: Logical reasoning; Sequencing; Identifying parts of a story

STORY ORDER

Look at the sentences in each box.
Think about the story they tell.
Write the number 1 next to the sentence that tells what happened first.
Write the number 2 next to the sentence that tells what happened second.
Write the number 3 next to the sentence that tells what happened third.

We made three big snowballs.

It snowed last night.

We put a hat on our snowman.

Tom gave the dog a bone.

The dog buried his bone.

The dog ran out the front door.

Skills: Logical reasoning; Sequencing; Identifying parts of a story

STORY ORDER

Look at the sentences in each box.
Think about the story they tell.
Write the number 1 next to the sentence that tells what happened first.
Write the number 2 next to the sentence that tells what happened second.
Write the number 3 next to the sentence that tells what happened third.

☐ Sam raked the leaves.

☐ Jan jumped into the pile of leaves.

☐ There was a big pile of leaves.

☐ The balloon popped!

☐ Joe blew up the balloon.

☐ Joe had a small balloon.

Skills: Logical reasoning; Sequencing; Identifying parts of a story

STORY ORDER

Look at the sentences in each box.
Think about the story they tell.
Write the number 1 next to the sentence that tells what happened first.
Write the number 2 next to the sentence that tells what happened second.
Write the number 3 next to the sentence that tells what happened third.

Jan made a card for Mom.

Jan got paper and scissors.

Jan cut out a big red heart.

The cat ran after the mouse.

A mouse was sitting outside the house.

The cat saw the mouse.

Skills: Logical reasoning; Sequencing; Identifying parts of a story

STORY ORDER

Look at the sentences in each box.
Think about the story they tell.
Write the number 1 next to the sentence that tells what happened first.
Write the number 2 next to the sentence that tells what happened second.
Write the number 3 next to the sentence that tells what happened third.

Dan pitched the ball to Pam.

The ball hit the window.

Pam's bat hit the ball.

We carried sand in a bucket.

Look at our sandcastle!

We brought our sand toys to the beach.

Skills: Logical reasoning; Sequencing; Identifying parts of a story

STORY ORDER

Look at the sentences in each box.
Think about the story they tell.
Write the number 1 next to the sentence that tells what happened first.
Write the number 2 next to the sentence that tells what happened second.
Write the number 3 next to the sentence that tells what happened third.

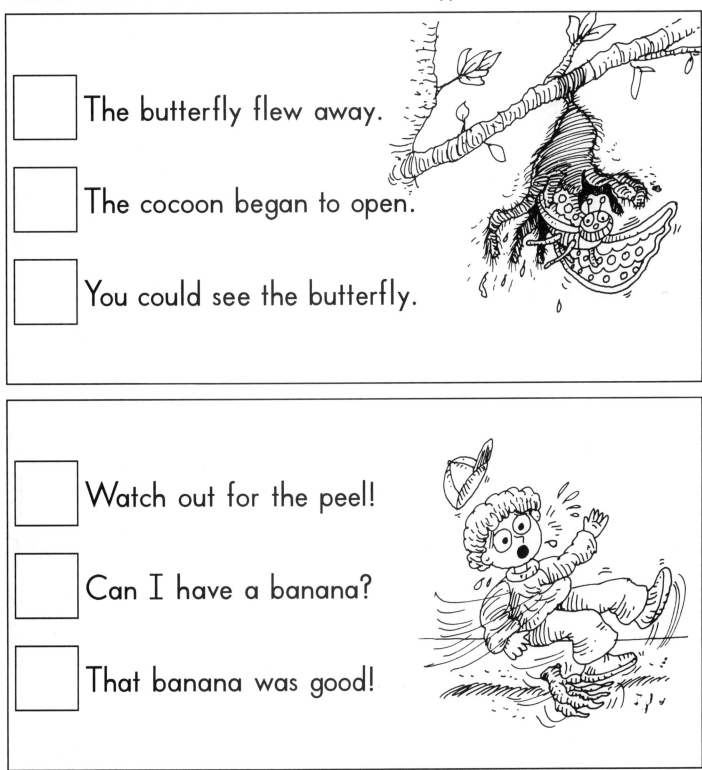

The butterfly flew away.

The cocoon began to open.

You could see the butterfly.

Watch out for the peel!

Can I have a banana?

That banana was good!

Skills: Logical reasoning; Sequencing; Identifying parts of a story

STORY ORDER

Look at the sentences in each box.
Think about the story they tell.
Write the number 1 next to the sentence that tells what happened first.
Write the number 2 next to the sentence that tells what happened second.
Write the number 3 next to the sentence that tells what happened third.

☐ Nan blew out the candles.

☐ Everyone sang *Happy Birthday.*

☐ Everyone ate cake.

☐ There was a knock on the door.

☐ Sue went out with Ann and Dave.

☐ Ann and Dave came in to get Sue.

Skills: Logical reasoning; Sequencing; Identifying parts of a story

STORY ORDER

Look at the sentences in each box.
Think about the story they tell.
Write the number 1 next to the sentence that tells what happened first.
Write the number 2 next to the sentence that tells what happened second.
Write the number 3 next to the sentence that tells what happened third.

The pirates dug for treasure.

The pirates counted the gold.

The pirates opened the old chest.

The bubble popped all over me.

I got a gumball!

I blew a giant bubble.

Skills: Logical reasoning; Sequencing; Identifying parts of a story

STORY ORDER

Look at the pictures below.
Think about what happened first.
Think about what happened next.
Tell a story about the pictures.
Have someone write it down in the space below.
Then color the pictures.

_____

_____

_____

_____

_____

_____

_____

Skills: Story order; Creative thinking; Telling a story using visual clues

STORY ORDER

Look at the pictures below.
Think about what happened first.
Think about what happened next.
Tell a story about the pictures.
Have someone write it down in the space below.
Then color the pictures.

Skills: Story order; Creative thinking; Telling a story using visual clues

STORY ORDER

Look at the pictures below.
Think about what happened first.
Think about what happened next.
Tell a story about the pictures.
Have someone write it down in the space below.
Then color the pictures.

_____

_____

_____

_____

_____

_____

_____

_____

Skills: Story order; Creative thinking; Telling a story using visual clues

STORY ORDER

Look at the pictures below.
Think about what happened first.
Think about what happened next.
Tell a story about the pictures.
Have someone write it down in the space below.
Then color the pictures.

_____
_____
_____

_____
_____
_____
_____

Skills: Story order; Creative thinking; Telling a story using visual clues

STORY ORDER

Look at the pictures below.
Think about what happened first.
Think about what happened next.
Tell a story about the pictures.
Have someone write it down in the space below.
Then color the pictures.

_____

_____

_____

_____

_____

_____

_____

_____

Skills: Story order; Creative thinking; Telling a story using visual clues

STORY ORDER

Look at the pictures.
Think about the story they tell.
Write the numbers 1, 2, 3, and 4 in the small boxes to put the story in order.
Then color the pictures.

Skills: Story order; Sequencing; Writing numerals

STORY ORDER

Look at the pictures.
Think about the story they tell.
Write the numbers 1, 2, 3, and 4 in the small boxes to put the story in order.
Then color the pictures.

Skills: Story order; Sequencing; Writing numerals

RHYMING WORDS

Look at each picture and say its name.
Draw lines to match the pictures whose names rhyme.

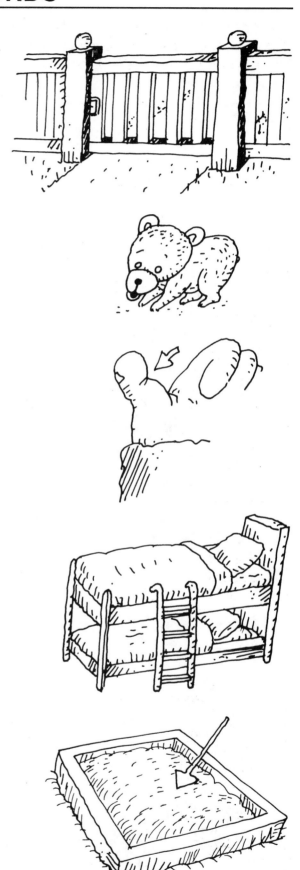

Skills: Understanding rhyme; Auditory discrimination; Recognizing sounds

RHYMING WORDS

Look at each picture and say its name.
Draw lines to match the pictures whose names rhyme.

Skills: Understanding rhyme; Auditory discrimination; Recognizing sounds

RHYMING WORDS

Look at each picture and say its name.
Draw lines to match the pictures whose names rhyme.

Skills: Understanding rhyme; Auditory discrimination; Recognizing sounds

133

RHYMING WORDS

Look at each picture and say its name.
Draw lines to match the pictures whose names rhyme.

RHYMING WORDS

Look at each picture and say its name.
Draw lines to match the pictures whose names rhyme.

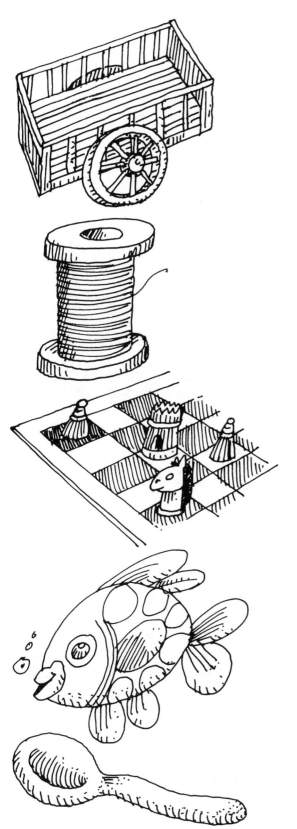

Skills: Understanding rhyme; Auditory discrimination; Recognizing sounds

RHYMING WORDS

Look at each slice of cake.
Say the name of the picture on each slice.
Color the slices with pictures whose names rhyme with cake.

Skills: Understanding rhyme; Auditory discrimination; Reproducing sounds

RHYMING WORDS

Look at the pictures on the turtle's shell.
Say the name of the picture on each part of the shell.
Color the parts of the shell with pictures whose names rhyme with shell.

Skills: Understanding rhyme; Auditory discrimination; Reproducing sounds

RHYMING WORDS

Look at the pictures on the blocks.
Say the name of the picture on each block.
Color the blocks with pictures whose names rhyme with block.

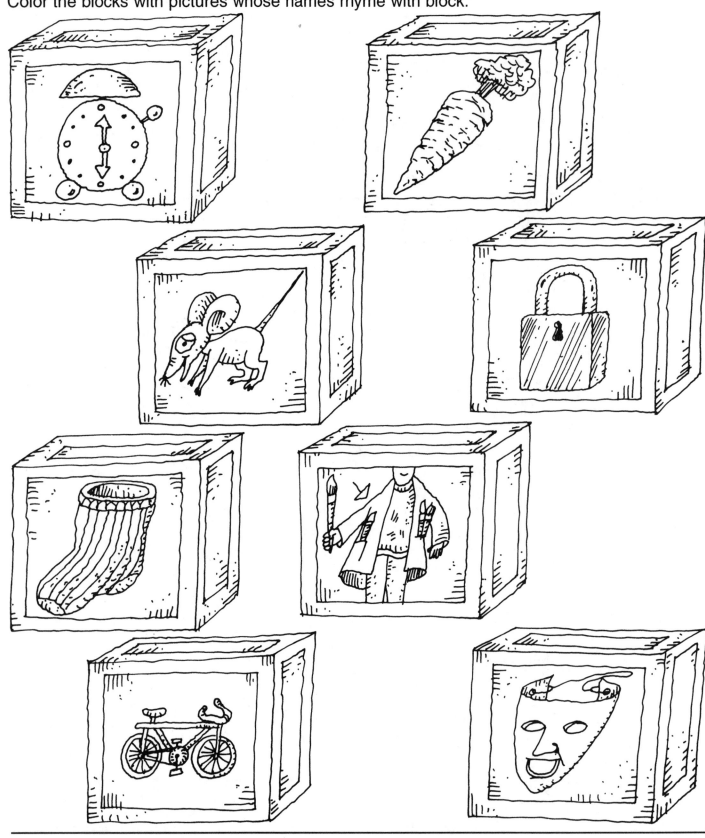

Skills: Understanding rhyme; Auditory discrimination; Reproducing sounds

RHYMING WORDS

Look at the trail below.
Say the name of the picture on each stone along the trail.
Color the stones in which the picture rhymes with trail.

Skills: Understanding rhyme; Auditory discrimination; Reproducing sounds

RHYMING WORDS

Look at the picture of the butterfly.
Look at the word in each section.
Find pairs of rhyming words.
Color the sections with rhyming words the same color.

yawn

part

hire

troop

witch

hum

deer

hole

thumb

loop

peer

lawn

pole

wire

pole

ditch

start

Skills: Identifying rhyming words; Auditory discrimination; Recognizing sounds

RHYMING WORDS

Look at the picture of the caterpillar.
Look at the word in each section.
Find pairs of rhyming words.
Color the sections with rhyming words the same color.

Skills: Identifying rhyming words; Auditory discrimination; Recognizing sounds

RHYMING WORDS

Look at the picture of the flower.
Look at the word in each section.
Find pairs of rhyming words.
Color the sections with rhyming words the same color.

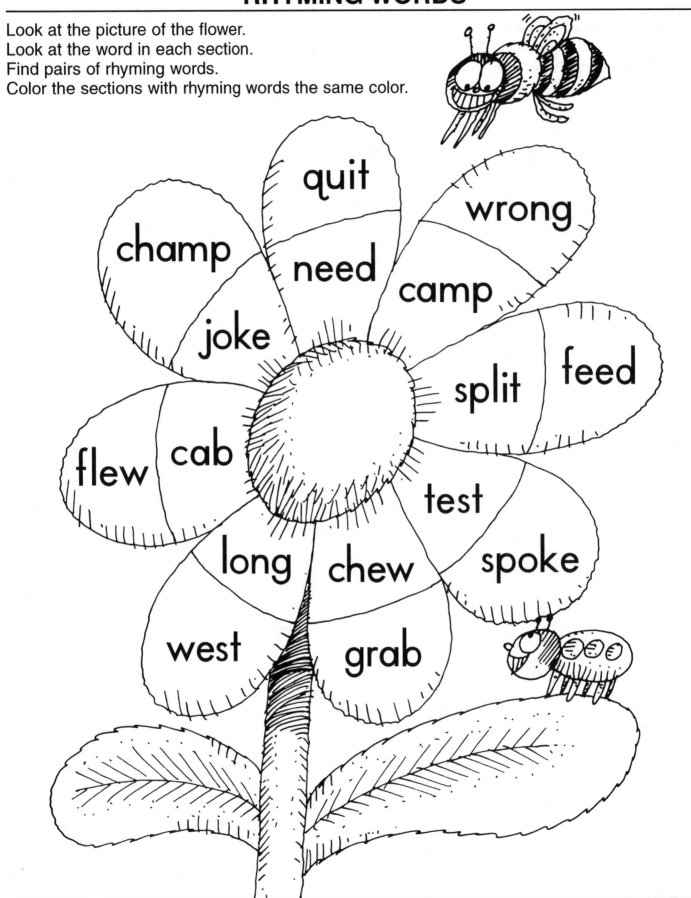

RHYMING WORDS

Look at the balloons on this page.
Look at the word in each balloon.
Find pairs of rhyming words.
Color the sections with rhyming words the same color.

Skills: Identifying rhyming words; Auditory discrimination; Recognizing sounds

RHYMING WORDS

Look at the first picture in each row and say its name.
Circle the picture whose name rhymes with it.

Skills: Recognizing rhyming words; Auditory discrimination

RHYMING WORDS

Look at the first picture in each row and say its name.
Circle the picture whose name rhymes with it.

Skills: Recognizing rhyming words; Auditory discrimination

RHYMING WORDS

Look at the first picture in each row and say its name.
Circle the picture whose name rhymes with it.

Skills: Recognizing rhyming words; Auditory discrimination

RHYMING WORDS

Look at the first picture in each row and say its name.
Circle the picture whose name rhymes with it.

Skills: Recognizing rhyming words; Auditory discrimination

RHYMING WORDS

Look at the first picture in each row and say its name.
Circle the picture whose name rhymes with it.

Skills: Recognizing rhyming words; Auditory discrimination

RHYMING WORDS

Look at the first picture in each row and say its name.
Circle the picture whose name rhymes with it.

Skills: Recognizing rhyming words; Auditory discrimination

RHYMING WORDS

Look at the first picture in each row and say its name.
Circle the picture whose name rhymes with it.

Skills: Recognizing rhyming words; Auditory discrimination

REASONING SKILLS

Look at the picture.
Circle five things that do not belong.
Then color the picture.

Skills: Visual discrimination; Logical reasoning; Inference

REASONING SKILLS

Look at the picture.
Circle five things that do not belong.
Then color the picture.

Skills: Visual discrimination; Logical reasoning; Inference

REASONING SKILLS

Look at the picture.
Circle five things that do not belong.
Then color the picture.

Skills: Visual discrimination; Logical reasoning; Inference

REASONING SKILLS

Look at the picture.
Circle five things that do not belong.
Then color the picture.

Skills: Visual discrimination; Logical reasoning; Inference

REASONING SKILLS

Look at the picture.
Circle five things that do not belong.
Then color the picture.

Skills: Visual discrimination; Logical reasoning; Inference

REASONING SKILLS

Look at the person at the beginning of each row.
Circle the picture that shows what each person uses.

Skills: Association; Logical reasoning

REASONING SKILLS

Look at the person at the beginning of each row.
Circle the picture that shows what each person uses.

Skills: Association; Logical reasoning

REASONING SKILLS

Look at the person at the beginning of each row.
Circle the picture that shows what each person uses.

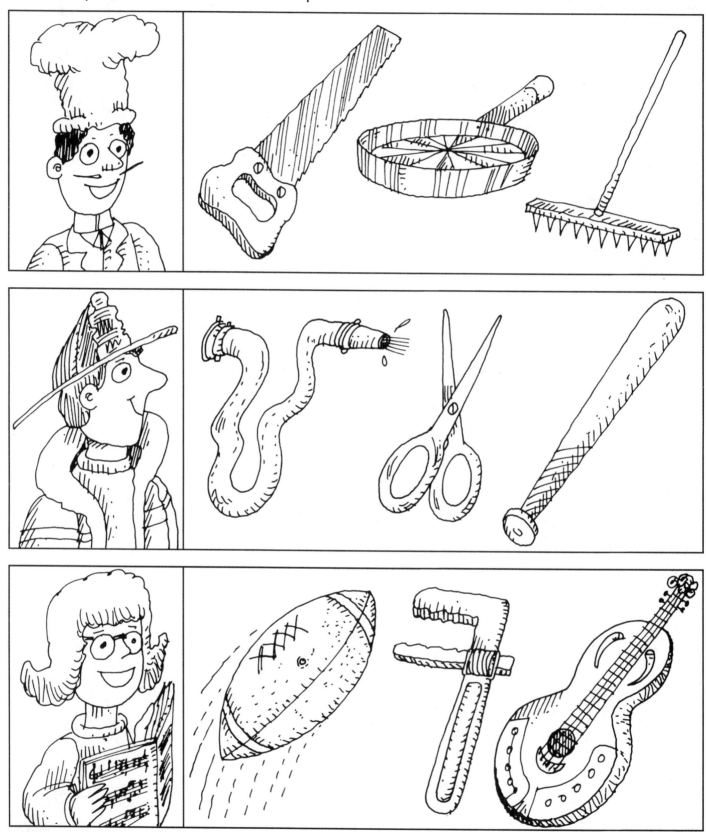

Skills: Association; Logical reasoning

REASONING SKILLS

Look at the picture at the beginning of each row.
Look at the row of pictures beside it.
Circle the picture that is like the first picture but facing a different direction.

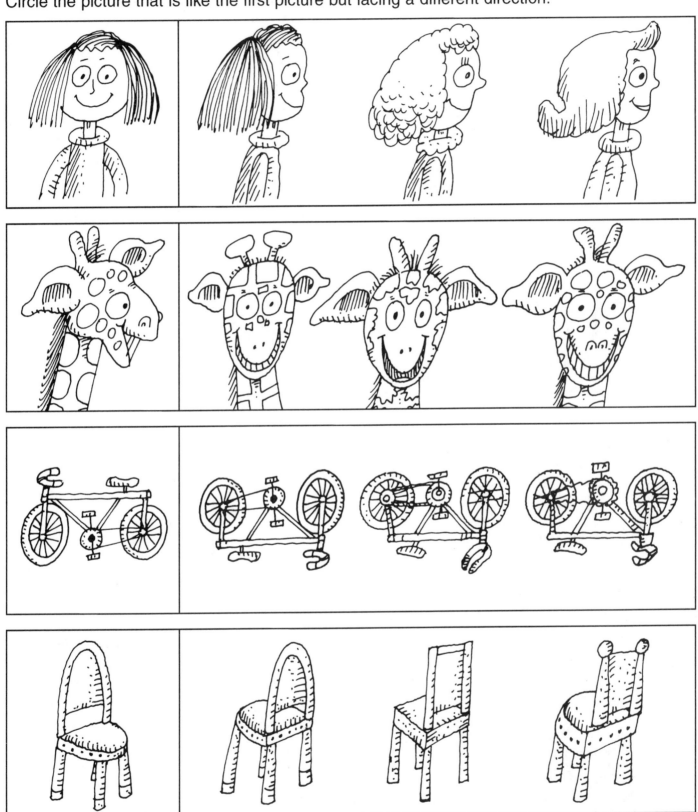

Skills: Inference; Visual discrimination; Spatial relations

REASONING SKILLS

Look at the picture at the beginning of each row.
Look at the row of pictures beside it.
Circle the picture that is like the first picture but in a different position.

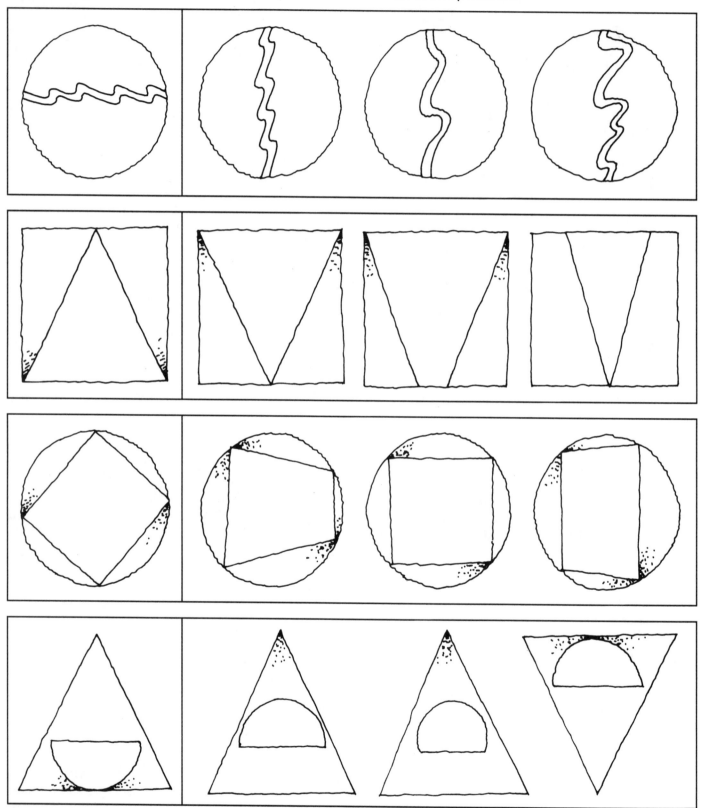

Skills: Inference; Visual discrimination; Spatial relations

REASONING SKILLS

Five children went to the park.
Look at the pictures and read the sentences.
Draw a line to show who each child is.

Pam   Joe   Deb   Dan   Sal

Pam doesn't like to play jumprope.
Joe is on the climber.
Deb is with Dan.

Skills: Inference; Deductive reasoning

REASONING SKILLS

Five children went to the movies.
Look at the pictures and read the sentences.
Draw a line to show who each child is.

Greg   Jake   Jess   Ali   Dana

Greg sat beside Dana.
Jake sat at the end of the row.
Ali sat in the middle.
Greg had popcorn.

Skills: Inference; Deductive reasoning

REASONING SKILLS

Everybody in the pool!
Look at the pictures and read the sentences.
Draw a line to show who each child is.

Tom   Sara   Pat   Jen   Sam

Sam likes to dive.
Tom and Jen play together.
Pat doesn't know how to swim.

Skills: Inference; Deductive reasoning

REASONING SKILLS

Look at the pictures and read the sentences.
Draw a line to show who each dog is.

Sam   Ollie   Cassie

Sue has three dogs.
She is training them to beg, fetch, and roll over.
Cassie can beg for a treat.
Sammy can fetch but doesn't beg.
Ollie can't fetch or beg.

Skills: Inference; Deductive reasoning

REASONING SKILLS

Look at the pictures and read the sentences.
Draw a line to show what kind of sandwich each child will eat.

peanut butter   tuna   cheese

Mom made sandwiches: one cheese,
one tuna, and one peanut butter.
Amy likes only tuna.
Nate likes all three sandwiches.
Jan likes cheese but not peanut butter.

Skills: Inference; Deductive reasoning

LETTER CONCEPTS

Look at the letters on this page.
Trace each letter.

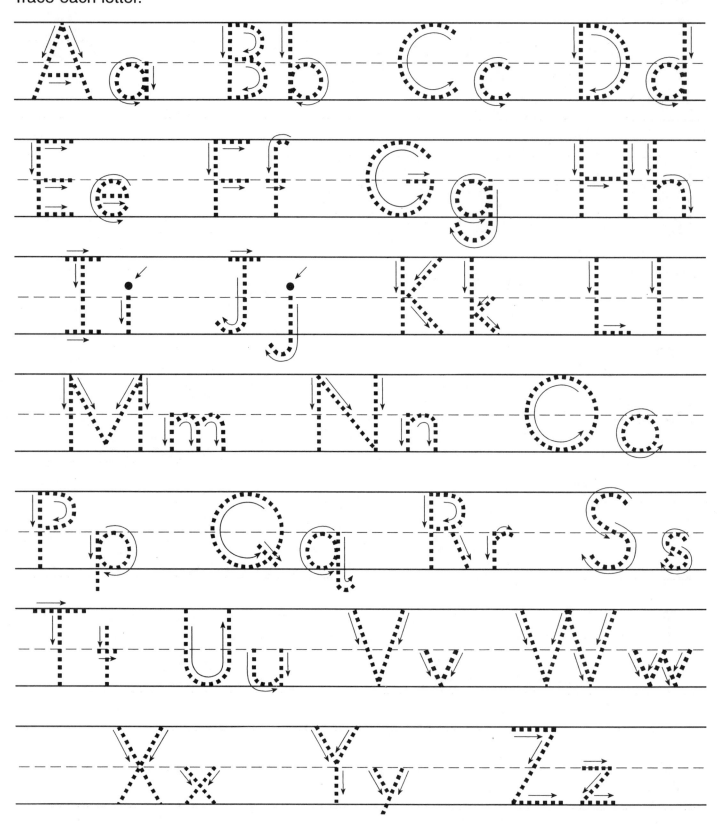

Skills: Letter order; Recognition of uppercase and lowercase letters; Fine motor skill development

LETTER CONCEPTS

Look at the letters from **A** to **Z**.
Trace each letter.
Then write that letter in the empty space beside it.

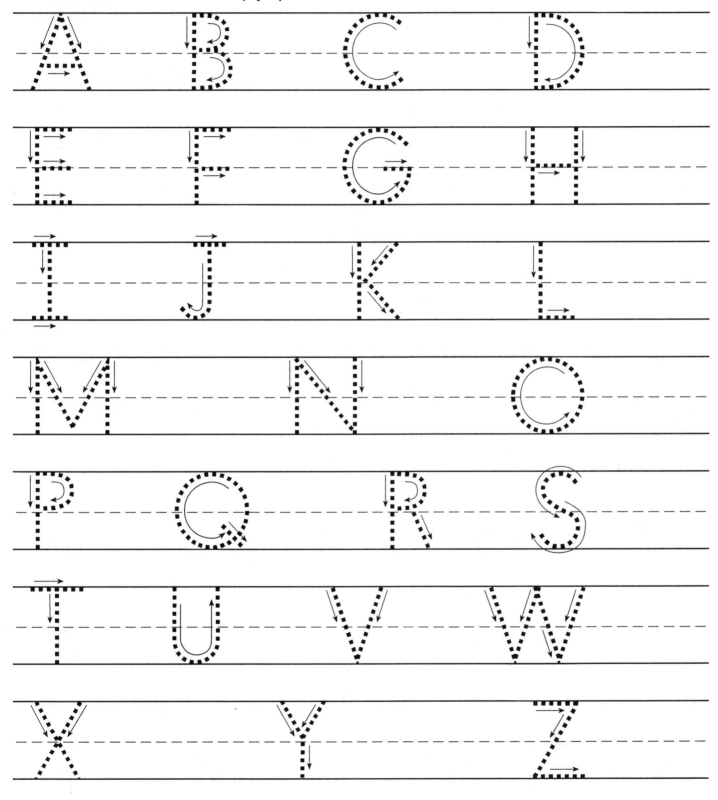

Skills: Letter order; Recognition of uppercase letters; Fine motor skill development

LETTER CONCEPTS

Look at the letters from **a** to **z**.
Trace each letter.
Then write that letter in the empty space beside it.

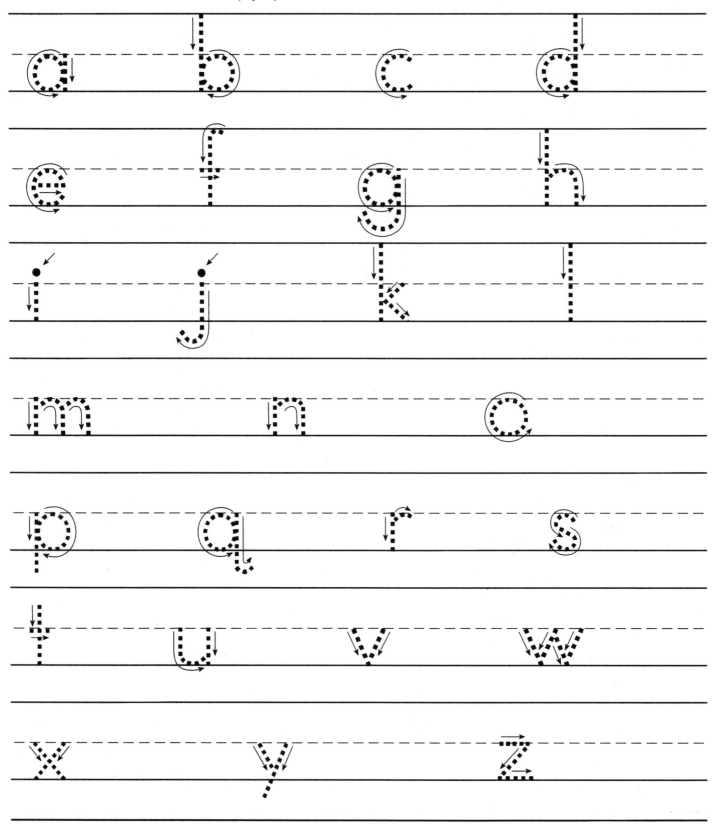

Skills: Letter order; Recognition of lowercase letters; Fine motor skill development

LETTER CONCEPTS

Connect the dots from **A** to **Z** to find out who is swinging in the tree.
Then color the picture.

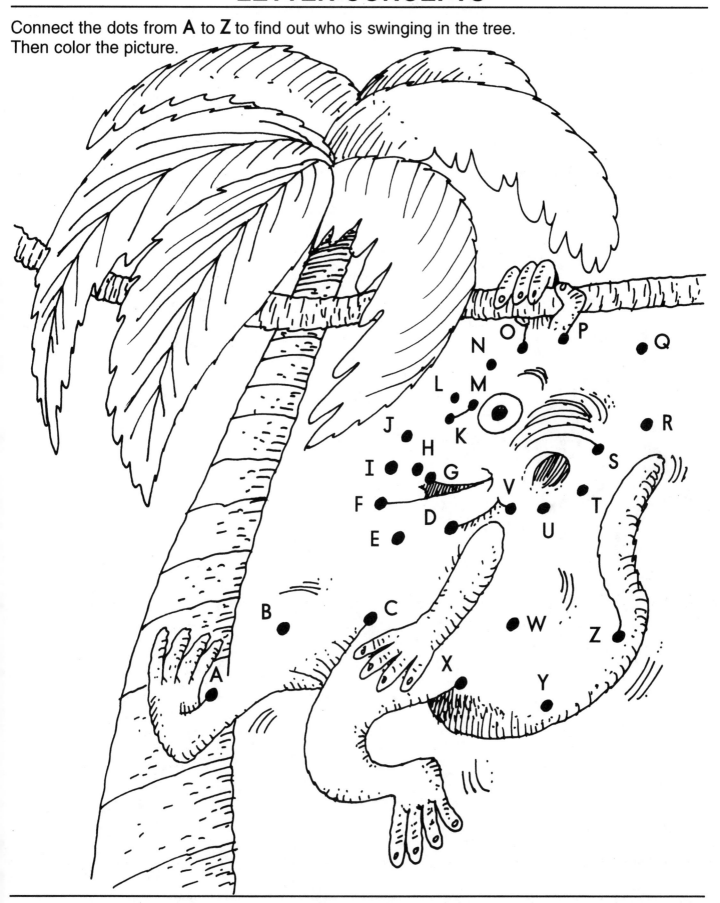

Skills: Letter order; Recognition lof uppercase letters

LETTER CONCEPTS

Connect the dots from **a** to **z** to find out who is swinging in the tree.
Then color the picture.

Skills: Letter order; Recognition of lowercase letters

LETTER CONCEPTS

Look at the pairs of sneakers.
Look at the letter in the sneaker on the left.
Write the letter that comes next in the other sneaker.

a b c d e f g h i j k l m n o p q r s t u v w x y z

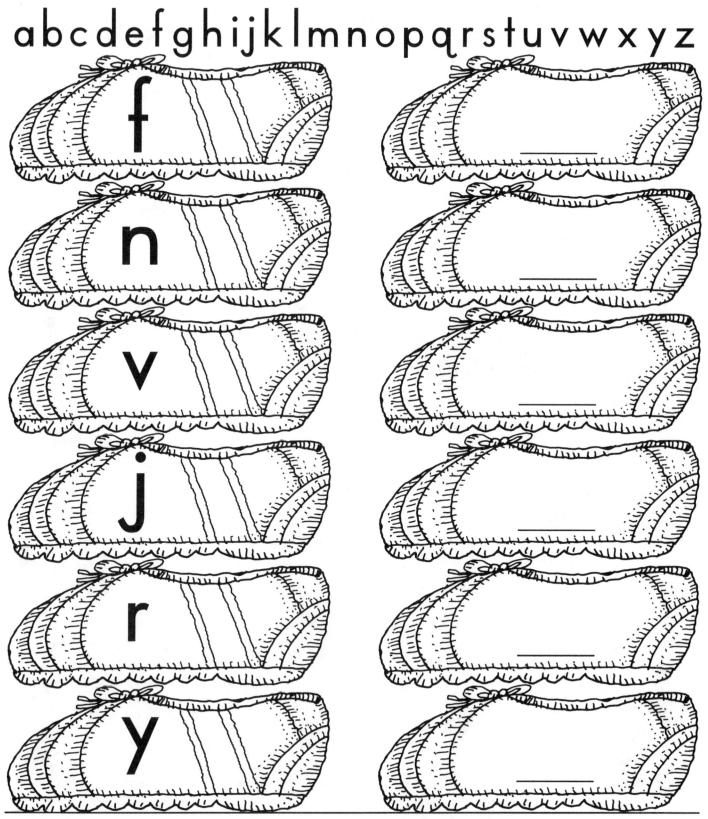

Skills: Letter order; Recognition of lowercase letters; Fine motor skill development

LETTER CONCEPTS

Look at the pairs of mittens.
Look at the letter in the mitten on the left.
Write the letter that comes next in the other mitten.

abcdefghijklmnopqrstuvwxyz

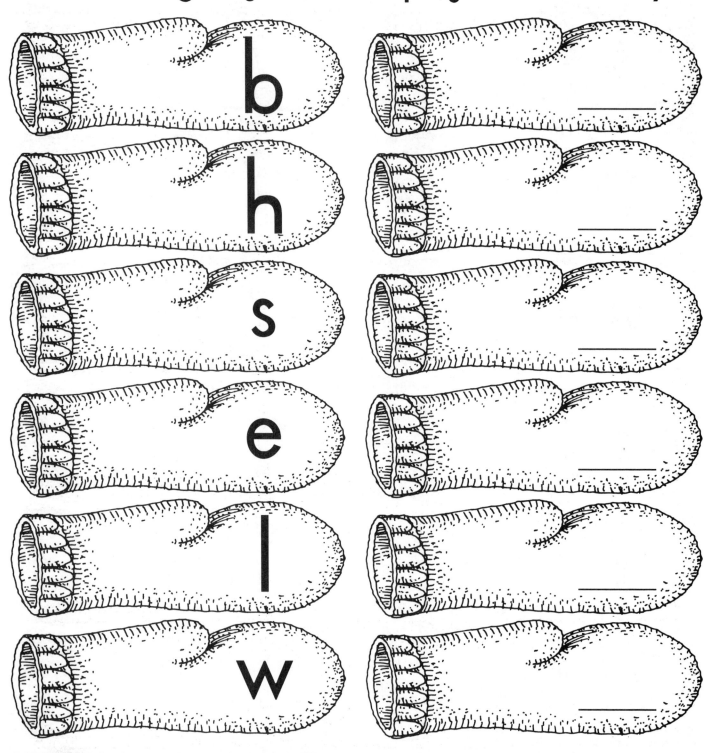

Skills: Letter order; Recognition of lowercase letters; Fine motor skill development

LETTER CONCEPTS

Look at the pairs of bookends.
Look at the letter in the bookend on the left.
Write the letter that comes next in the other bookend.

A B C D E F G H I J K L M N O P Q R S T U V W X Y Z

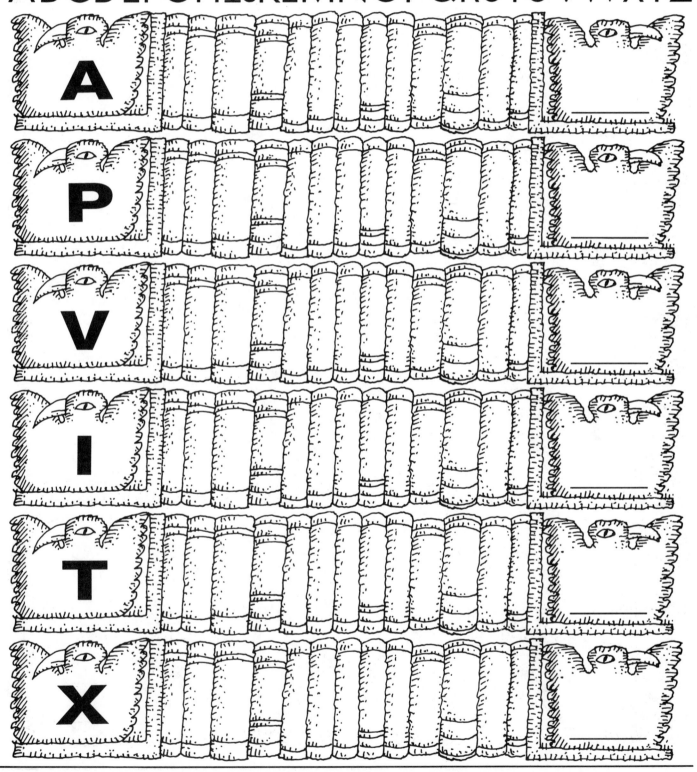

Skills: Letter order; Recognition of uppercase letters; Fine motor skill development

LETTER CONCEPTS

Look at the butterfly's wings.
Look at the letter in the wing on the left.
Write the letter that comes next in the other wing.

ABCDEFGHIJKLMNOPQRSTUVWXYZ

Skills: Letter order; Recognition of uppercase letters; Fine motor skill development

LETTER CONCEPTS

Look at each pair of eyeglasses.
Look at the letter in the lens on the right.
Write the letter that comes before in the other lens.

a b c d e f g h i j k l m n o p q r s t u v w x y z

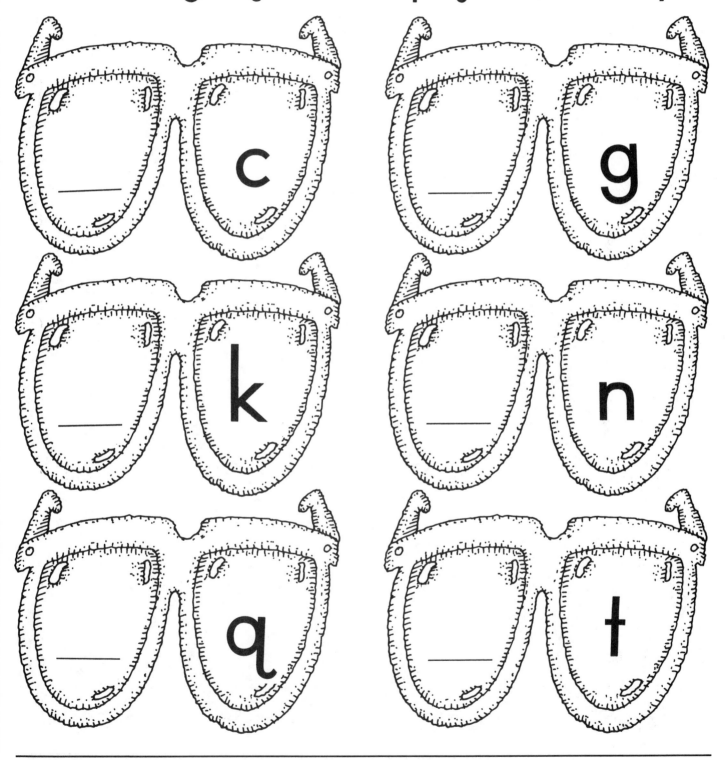

Skills: Letter order; Recognition of lowercase letters; Fine motor skill development

LETTER CONCEPTS

Look at each pair of earrings.
Look at the letter in the earring on the right.
Write the letter that comes before in the other earring.

a b c d e f g h i j k l m n o p q r s t u v w x y z

LETTER CONCEPTS

Look at each pair of socks.
Look at the letter in the sock on the right.
Write the letter that comes before in the other sock.

ABCDEFGHIJKLMNOPQRSTUVWXYZ

Skills: Letter order; Recognition of uppercase letters; Fine motor skill development

LETTER CONCEPTS

Look at each pair of shoes.
Look at the letter in the shoe on the right.
Write the letter that comes before in the other shoe.

ABCDEFGHIJKLMNOPQRSTUVWXYZ

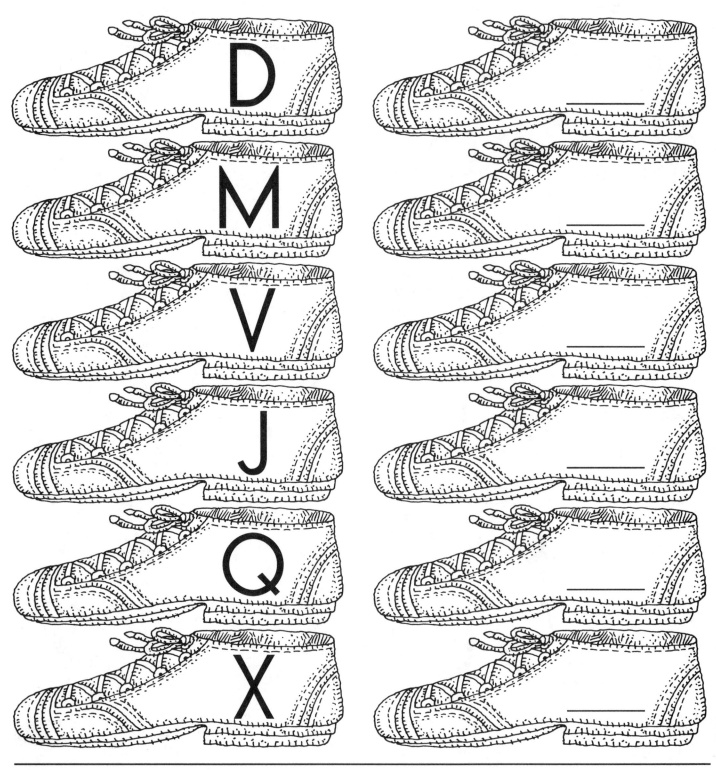

Skills: Letter order; Recognition lof uppercase letters; Fine motor skill development

LETTER CONCEPTS

Look at each necklace.
Fill in the missing letters.

a b c d e f g h i j k l m n o p q r s t u v w x y z

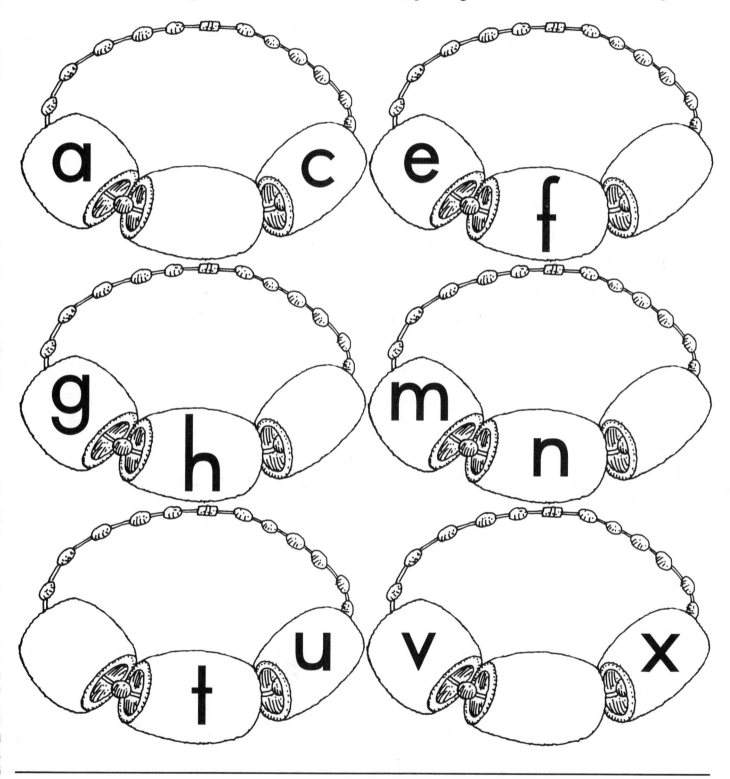

Skills: Letter order; Recognition of lowercase letters; Fine motor skill development

LETTER CONCEPTS

Look at each train.
Fill in the missing letters.

abcdefghijklmnopqrstuvwxyz

Skills: Letter order; Recognition of lowercase letters; Fine motor skill development

LETTER CONCEPTS

Look at each caterpillar.
Fill in the missing letters.

abcdefghijklmnopqrstuvwxyz

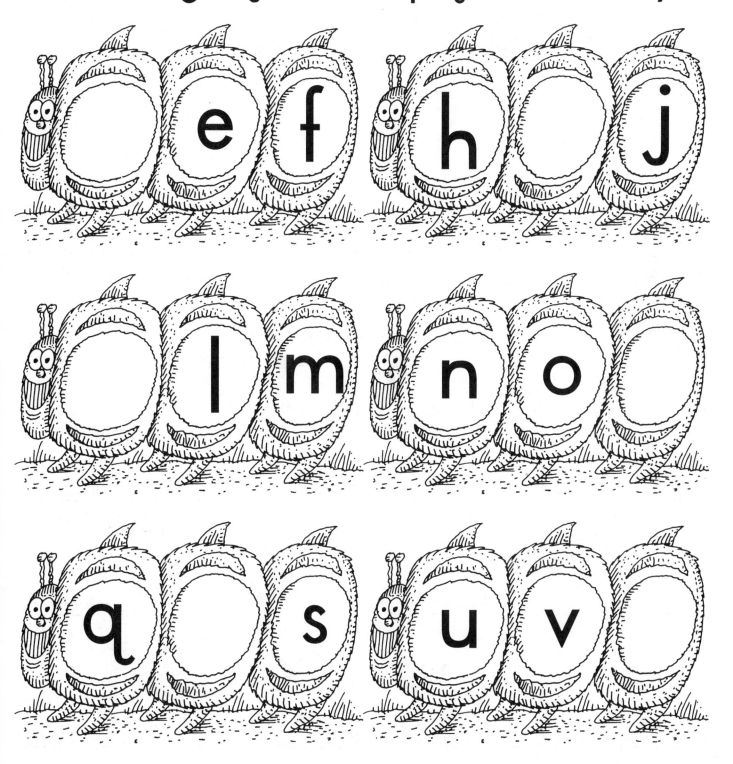

Skills: Letter order; Recognition of lowercase letters; Fine motor skill development

LETTER CONCEPTS

Look at the path through the forest.
Fill in the missing letters from **a** to **z**.

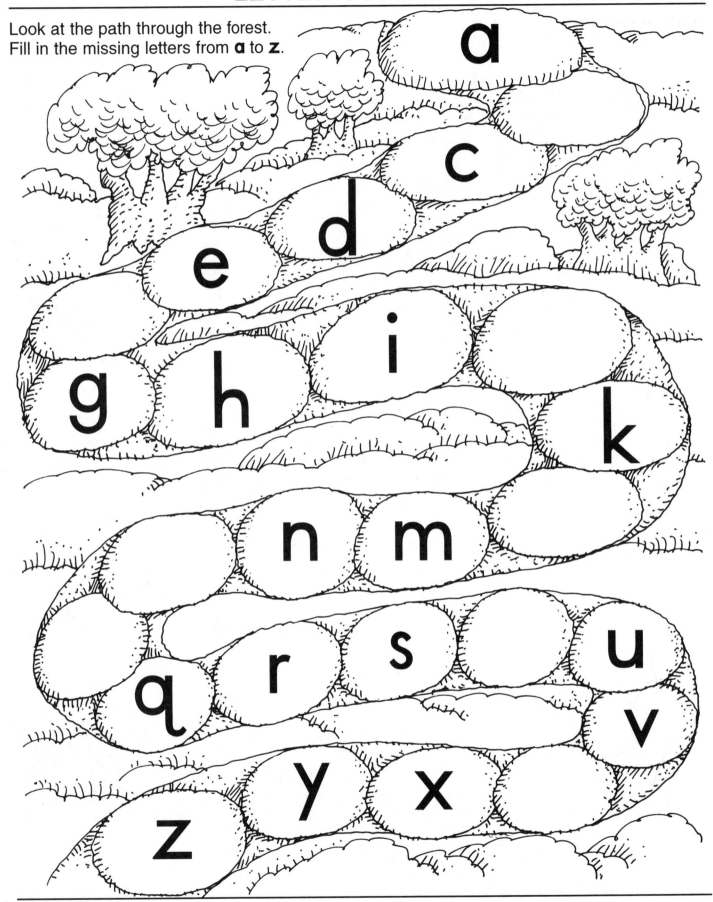

Skills: Letter order; Recognition of lowercase letters; Fine motor skill development

LETTER CONCEPTS

Look at the stars in the sky.
Fill in the missing letters from **A** to **Z**.

Skills: Letter order; Recognition of uppercase letters; Fine motor skill development

LETTER CONCEPTS

Look at the chalkboard in the classroom.
Someone wrote the alphabet out of order.
Cross out the letters that are in the wrong place.
Then write the alphabet correctly in the space below.

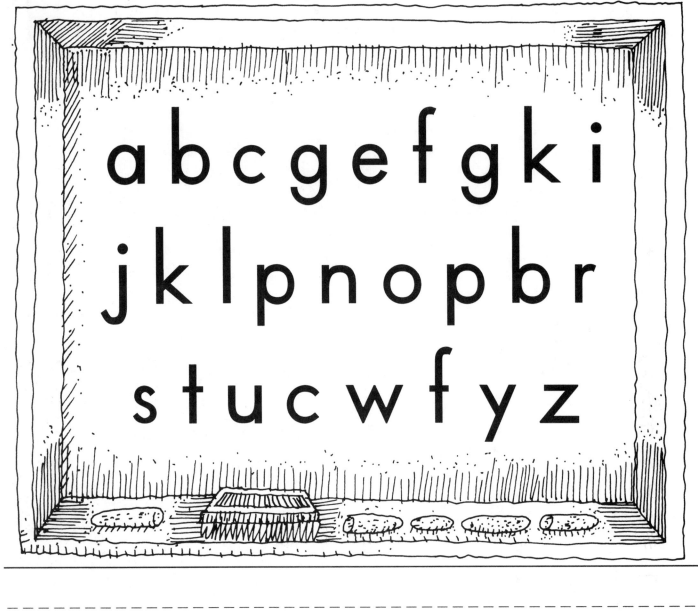

Skills: Letter order; Recognition of lowercase letters; Fine motor skill development

LETTER CONCEPTS

Look at the picture below.
The letters A to M are hidden in the picture.
Say the letters in order and circle each letter you see.
Then write the first part of the alphabet correctly in the space below.

Skills: Letter order; Recognition of uppercase letters; Fine motor skill development

LETTER CONCEPTS

Look at the picture below.
The letters **N** to **Z** are hidden in the picture.
Say the letters in order and circle each letter you see.
Then write the last part of the alphabet correctly in the space below.

- -

_____

- -

_____

- -

_____

Skills: Letter order; Recognition of uppercase letters; Fine motor skill development

PHONICS

Initial consonant: **b**

Baby begins with a **b**.
Look at the pictures.
Color the ones whose names begin with a **b**.

Skills: Recognition of the initial consonant "b"; Sound/symbol association; Auditory discrimination

PHONICS

Initial consonant: **c**

Cat begins with a **c**.
Look at the pictures.
Color the ones whose names begin with a **c**.

Skills: Recognition of the initial consonant "c"; Sound/symbol association; Auditory discrimination

PHONICS

Initial consonant: **d**

Dog begins with a **d**.
Look at the pictures.
Color the ones whose names begin with a **d**.

Skills: Recognition of the initial consonant "d"; Sound/symbol association; Auditory discrimination

PHONICS

Initial consonant: **f**

Fox begins with an **f**.
Look at the pictures.
Color the ones whose names begin with an **f**.

Skills: Recognition of the initial consonant "f"; Sound/symbol association; Auditory discrimination

PHONICS

Initial consonant: **g**

Gum begins with a **g**.
Look at the pictures.
Color the ones whose names begin with a **g**.

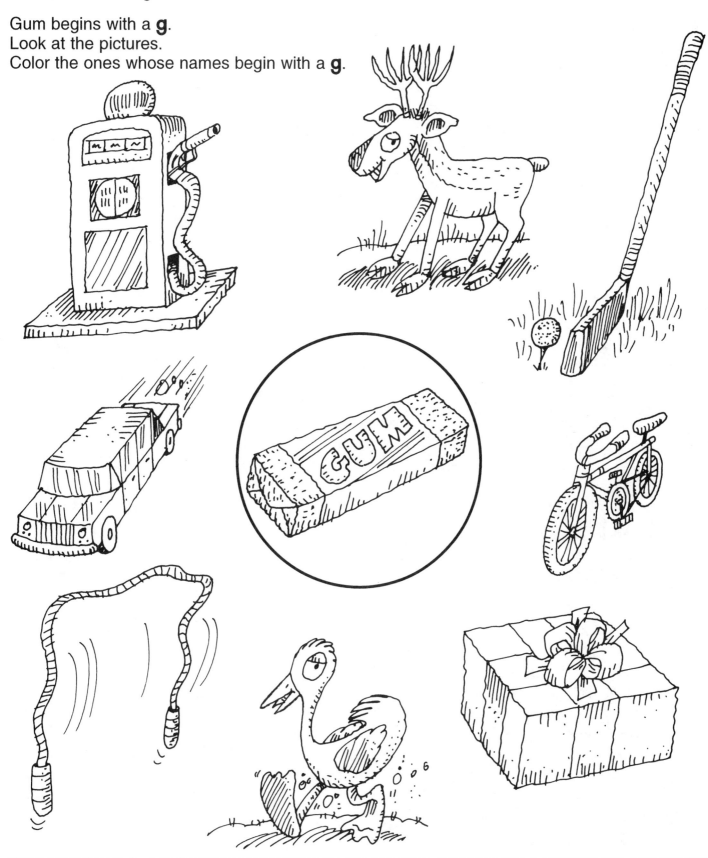

Skills: Recognition of the initial consonant "g"; Sound/symbol association; Auditory discrimination

PHONICS

Initial consonant: **h**

Hat begins with an **h**.
Look at the pictures.
Color the ones whose names begin with an **h**.

Skills: Recognition of the initial consonant "h"; Sound/symbol association; Auditory discrimination

PHONICS

Initial consonant: **j**

Jet begins with a **j**.
Look at the pictures.
Color the ones whose names begin with a **j**.

Skills: Recognition of the initial consonant "j"; Sound/symbol association; Auditory discrimination

PHONICS

Initial consonant: **k**

Key begins with a **k**.
Look at the pictures.
Color the ones whose names begin with a **k**.

Skills: Recognition of the initial consonant "k"; Sound/symbol association; Auditory discrimination

PHONICS

Initial consonant: l

Lemon begins with an l.
Look at the pictures.
Color the ones whose names begin with an l.

Skills: Recognition of the initial consonant "l"; Sound/symbol association; Auditory discrimination

PHONICS

Initial consonant: **m**

Mask begins with an **m**.
Look at the pictures.
Color the ones whose names begin with an **m**.

Skills: Recognition of the initial consonant "m"; Sound/symbol association; Auditory discrimination

PHONICS

Initial consonant: **n**

Net begins with an **n**.
Look at the pictures.
Color the ones whose names begin with an **n**.

Skills: Recognition of the initial consonant "n"; Sound/symbol association; Auditory discrimination

PHONICS

Initial consonant: **p**

Pumpkin begins with a **p**.
Look at the pictures.
Color the ones whose names begin with a **p**.

Skills: Recognition of the initial consonant "p"; Sound/symbol association; Auditory discrimination

PHONICS

Initial consonant: **q**

Quack begins with a **q**.
Look at the pictures.
Color the ones whose names begin with a **q**.

Skills: Recognition of the initial consonant "q"; Sound/symbol association; Auditory discrimination

PHONICS

Initial consonant: **r**

Rain begins with an **r**.
Look at the pictures.
Color the ones whose names begin with an **r**.

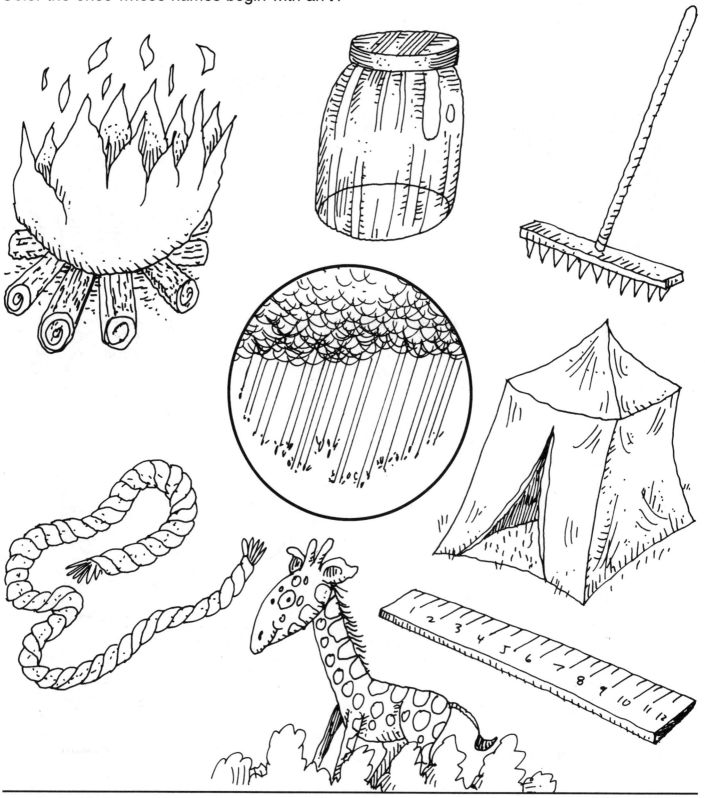

Skills: Recognition of the initial consonant "r"; Sound/symbol association; Auditory discrimination

PHONICS

Initial consonant: **s**

Seesaw begins with an **s**.
Look at the pictures.
Color the ones whose names begin with an **s**.

Skills: Recognition of the initial consonant "s"; Sound/symbol association; Auditory discrimination

PHONICS

Initial consonant: **t**

Tomato begins with a **t**.
Look at the pictures.
Color the ones whose names begin with a **t**.

Skills: Recognition of the initial consonant "t"; Sound/symbol association; Auditory discrimination

PHONICS

Initial consonant: **v**

Vegetable begins with a **v**.
Look at the pictures.
Color the ones whose names begin with a **v**.

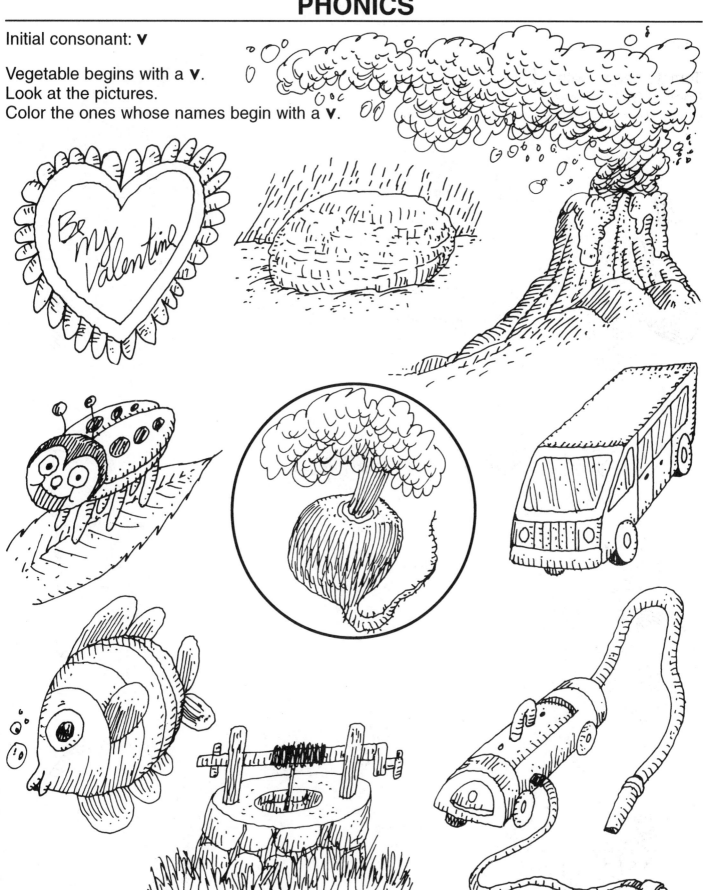

Skills: Recognition of the initial consonant "v"; Sound/symbol association; Auditory discrimination

PHONICS

Initial consonant: **w**

Worm begins with a **w**.
Look at the pictures.
Color the ones whose names begin with a **w**.

Skills: Recognition of the initial consonant "w"; Sound/symbol association; Auditory discrimination

PHONICS

Initial consonant: **y**

Yell begins with a **y**.
Look at the pictures.
Color the ones whose names begin with a **y**.

Skills: Recognition of the initial consonant "y"; Sound/symbol association; Auditory discrimination

PHONICS

Initial consonant: **z**

Zinnia begins with a **z**.
Look at the pictures.
Color the ones whose names begin with a **z**.

Skills: Recognition of the initial consonant "z"; Sound/symbol association; Auditory discrimination

PHONICS

Look at the pictures below.
Write the letter that makes the sound you hear at the beginning of each word.
Then color the pictures.

PHONICS

Look at the pictures below.
Write the letter that makes the sound you hear at the beginning of each word.
Then color the pictures.

Skills: Recognition of the initial consonants; Sound/symbol association; Writing letters;
Auditory discrimination

PHONICS

Final consonants: **d** and **g**

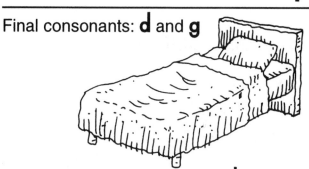

The ending sound in bed is a **d**. The ending sound in bag is a **g**.
Look at the picture in the first box of each row.
Color the pictures that end with the same sound.

Skills: Recognition of the final consonants "d" and "g"; Sound/symbol association; Auditory discrimination

PHONICS

Final consonants: **b** and **t**

The ending sound in web is a **b**. The ending sound in goat is a **t**.
Look at the picture in the first box of each row.
Color the pictures that end with the same sound.

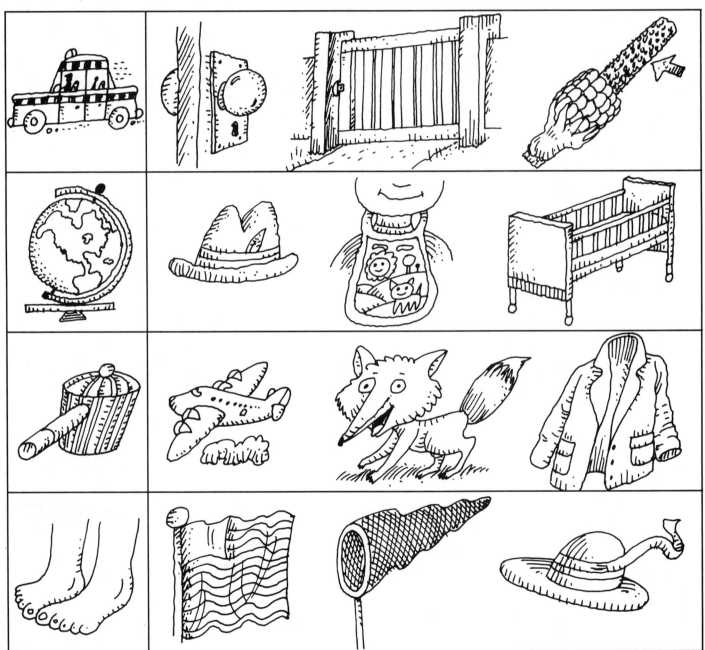

Skills: Recognition of the final consonants "b" and "t"; Sound/symbol association; Auditory discrimination

PHONICS

Final consonants: **f** and **k**

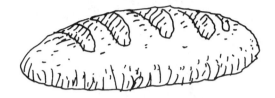

The ending sound in loaf is an **f**. The ending sound in lock is a **k**.
Look at the picture in the first box of each row.
Color the pictures that end with the same sound.

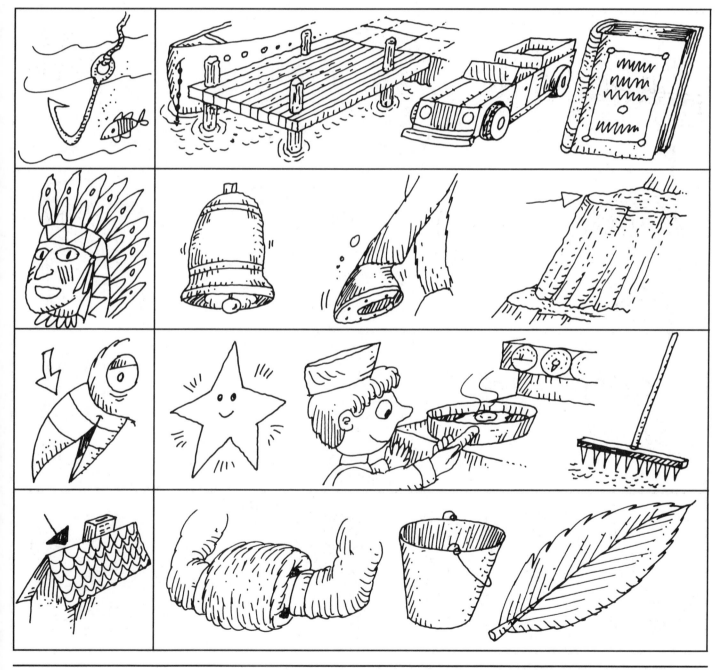

Skills: Recognition of the final consonants "f" and "k"; Sound/symbol association; Auditory discrimination

PHONICS

Final consonants: **l** and **m**

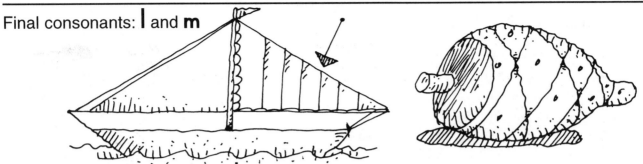

The ending sound in sail is an **l**. The ending sound in ham is an **m**.
Look at the picture in the first box of each row.
Color the pictures that end with the same sound.

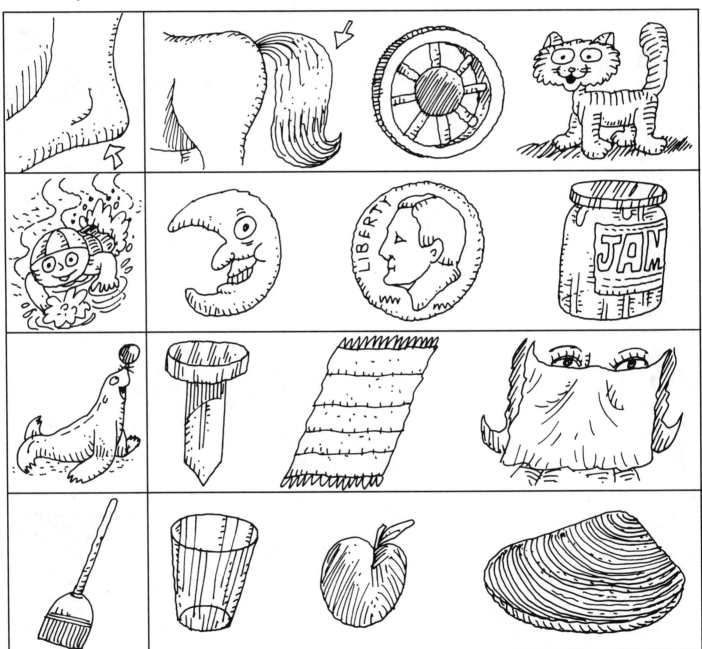

Skills: Recognition of the final consonants "l" and "m"; Sound/symbol association; Auditory discrimination

PHONICS

Final consonants: **n** and **p**

The ending sound in hen is an **n**. The ending sound in jeep is a **p**.
Look at the picture in the first box of each row.
Color the pictures that end with the same sound.

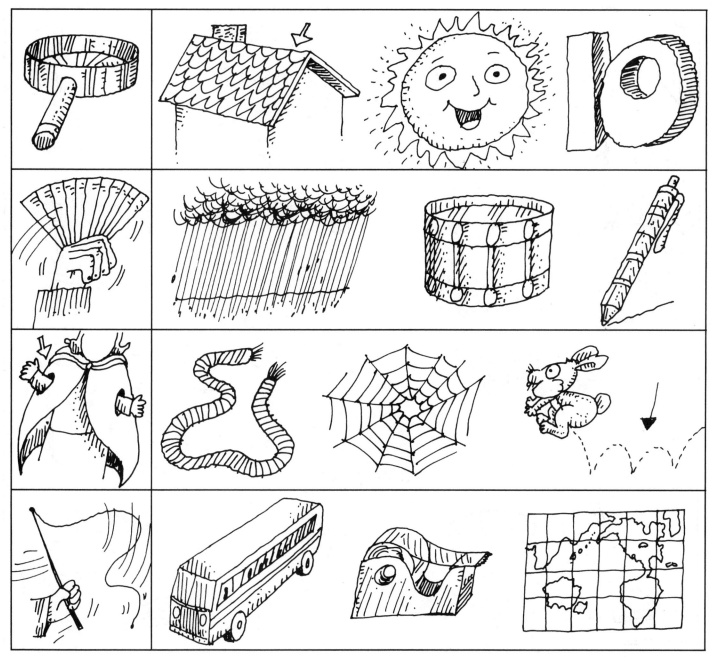

Skills: Recognition of the final consonants "n" and "p"; Sound/symbol association; Auditory discrimination

213

PHONICS

Final consonants: **r** and **v**

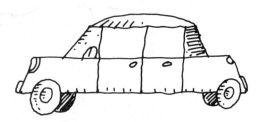 

The ending sound in car is an **r**. The ending sound in dove is a **v**.
Look at the picture in the first box of each row.
Color the pictures that end with the same sound.

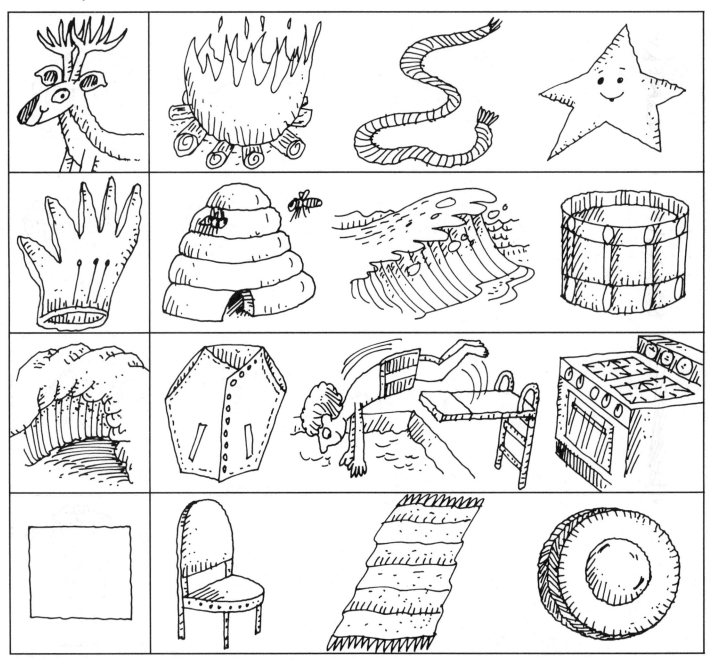

Skills: Recognition of the final consonants "r" and "v"; Sound/symbol association; Auditory discrimination

PHONICS

Final consonants: **ll** and **ss**

The ending sound in well is **ll**. The ending sound in mess is **ss**.
Look at the picture in the first box of each row.
Color the pictures that end with the same sound.

Skills: Recognition of the final consonants "ll" and "ss"; Sound/symbol association; Auditory discrimination

PHONICS

Look at the pictures below.
Write the letter that makes the sound you hear at the end of each word.
Then color the pictures.

PHONICS

Look at the pictures below.
Write the letter that makes the sound you hear at the end of each word.
Then color the pictures.

Skills: Recognition of final consonants; Sound/symbol association; Writing letters; Auditory discrimination

PHONICS

Short vowel: ă

Bag has the short **a** sound.
Look at the picture on each bag.
Color the pictures that have the short **a** sound.

Skills: Recognition of the short vowel "a"; Sound/symbol association; Auditory discrimination

PHONICS

Short vowel: ĕ

Bell has the short **e** sound.
Look at the picture in each bell.
Color the pictures that have the short **e** sound.

Skills: Recognition of the short vowel "e"; Sound/symbol association; Auditory discrimination

PHONICS

Short vowel: ĭ

Bib has the short **i** sound.
Look at the picture in each bib.
Color the pictures that have the short **i** sound.

Skills: Recognition of the short vowel "i"; Sound/symbol association; Auditory discrimination

PHONICS

Short vowel: ŏ

Box has the short **o** sound.
Look at the picture in each box.
Color the pictures that have the short **o** sound.

Skills: Recognition of the short vowel "o"; Sound/symbol association; Auditory discrimination

221

PHONICS

Short vowel: ǔ

Rug has the short **u** sound.
Look at the picture in each rug.
Color the pictures that have the short **u** sound.

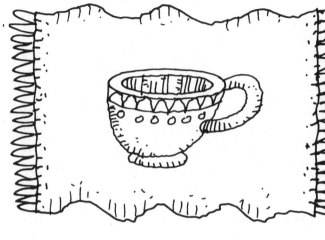

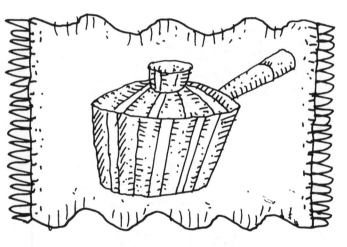

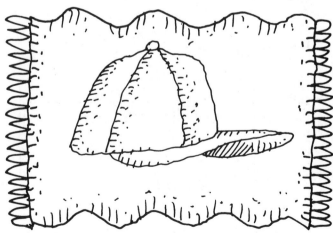

Skills: Recognition of the short vowel "u"; Sound/symbol association; Auditory discrimination

PHONICS

Long vowel: $\bar{a}$

Cake has the long **a** sound.
Look at the pictures on this page.
Color the pictures that have the long **a** sound.

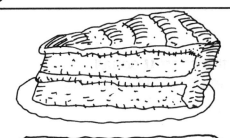

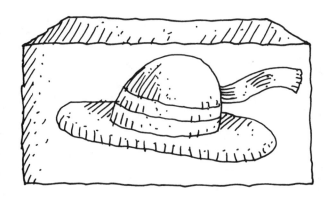

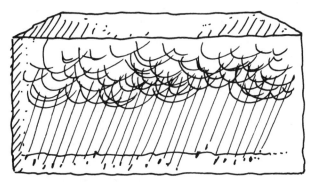

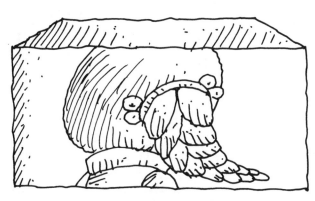

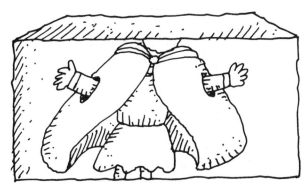

Skills: Recognition of the long vowel "a"; Sound/symbol association; Auditory discrimination

PHONICS

Long vowel: ē

Teeth has the long **e** sound.
Look at the pictures on this page.
Color the pictures that have the long **e** sound.

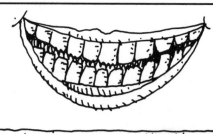

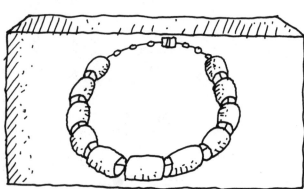
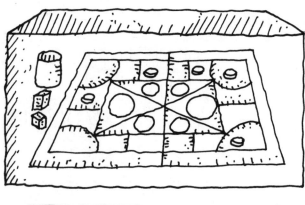

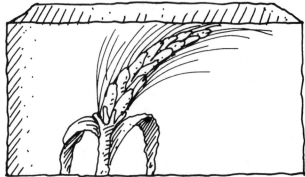
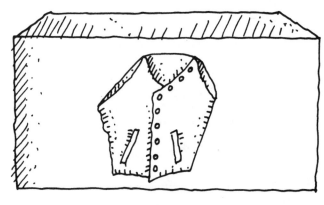
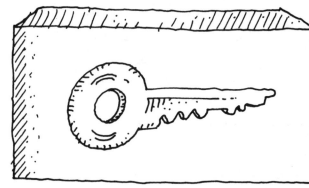

Skills: Recognition of the long vowel "e"; Sound/symbol association; Auditory discrimination

PHONICS

Long vowel: ī

Lime has the long **i** sound.
Look at the pictures on this page.
Color the pictures that have the long **i** sound.

Skills: Recognition of the long vowel "i"; Sound/symbol association; Auditory discrimination

PHONICS

Long vowel: ō

Goat has the long **o** sound.
Look at the pictures on this page.
Color the pictures that have the long **o** sound.

Skills: Recognition of the long vowel "o"; Sound/symbol association; Auditory discrimination

PHONICS

Long vowel: ū

Mule has the long **u** sound.
Look at the pictures on this page.
Color the pictures that have the long **u** sound.

Skills: Recognition of the long vowel "u"; Sound/symbol association; Auditory discrimination

PHONICS

Which ones have short vowel sounds?
Color them yellow.
Color the other pictures blue.

Skills: Recognition of short vowel sounds; Auditory discrimination

PHONICS

Which ones have long vowel sounds?
Color them green.
Color the other pictures red.

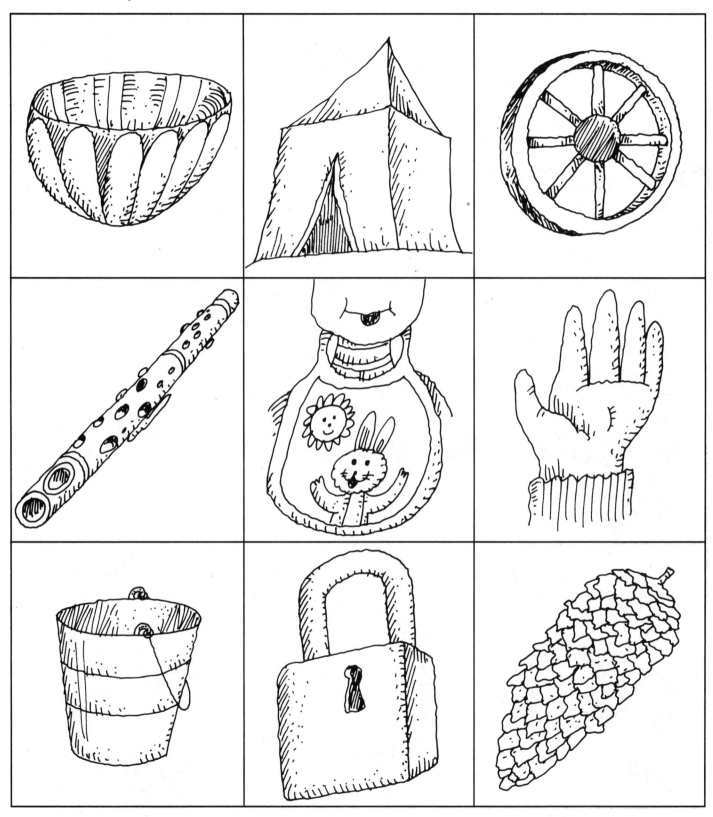

Skills: Recognition of long vowel sounds; Auditory discrimination

ABC ORDER

Look at the letters in the pails and shovels.
If the letter comes before P, color the picture blue.
If it comes after P, color the picture yellow.

Skills: Ordering uppercase and lowercase letters; Following directions

ABC ORDER

Look at the letters in the balloons.
If the letter comes before B, color the picture blue.
If it comes after B, color the picture yellow.

A   s   a

p   X   H

Z   b   J   t

m   U   e

w   l   A

Skills: Ordering uppercase and lowercase letters; Following directions

ABC ORDER

Look at the letters in the kites.
If the letter comes before **K**, color the picture blue.
If it comes after **K**, color the kite pink.

z

B

f

T

u

z

M

S

P

j

o

h

E

a

L

x

Skills: Ordering uppercase and lowercase letters; Following directions

ABC ORDER

Look at all the beads.
Look at the letter in each bead.
Write the missing letters to complete the alphabet.

Skills: Writing lowercase letters; Understanding letter order; Fine motor skill development

ABC ORDER

Look at all the bats.
Look at the letter in each wing.
Write a number in the other wing to put the bats in ABC order.

Skills: Using knowledge of letter order; Fine motor skill development

ABC ORDER

Look at all the butterflies.
Look at the letter in each butterfly's wing.
Write a number in the other wing to put the butterflies in ABC order.

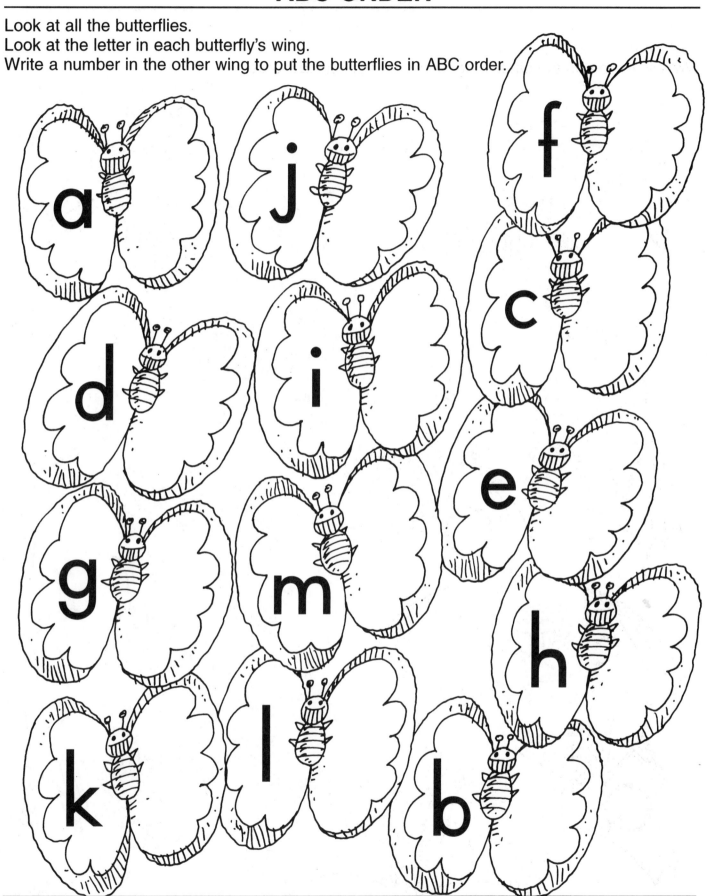

Skills: Using knowledge of letter order; Fine motor skill development

ABC ORDER

Look at the uppercase and lowercase letters in the paintbrushes and cans.
Color the ones that come first yellow.
Color the ones that come second orange.
Color the ones that come third red.
Color the ones that come fourth blue.

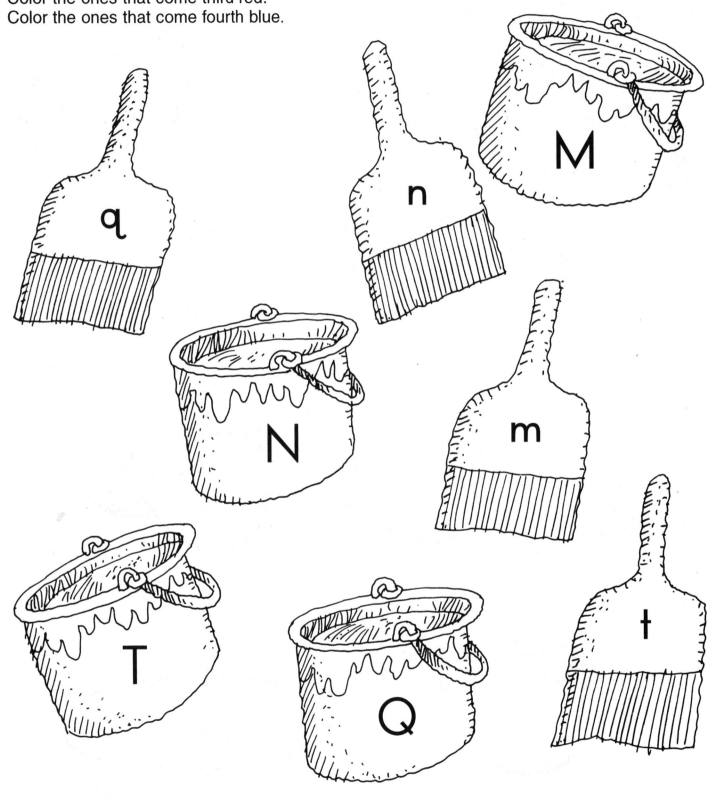

Skills: Ordering uppercase and lowercase letters; Following directions

ABC ORDER

Look at the uppercase and lowercase letters in the cups and saucers.
Color the ones that come first red.
Color the ones that come second blue.
Color the ones that come third green.
Color the ones that come fourth yellow.

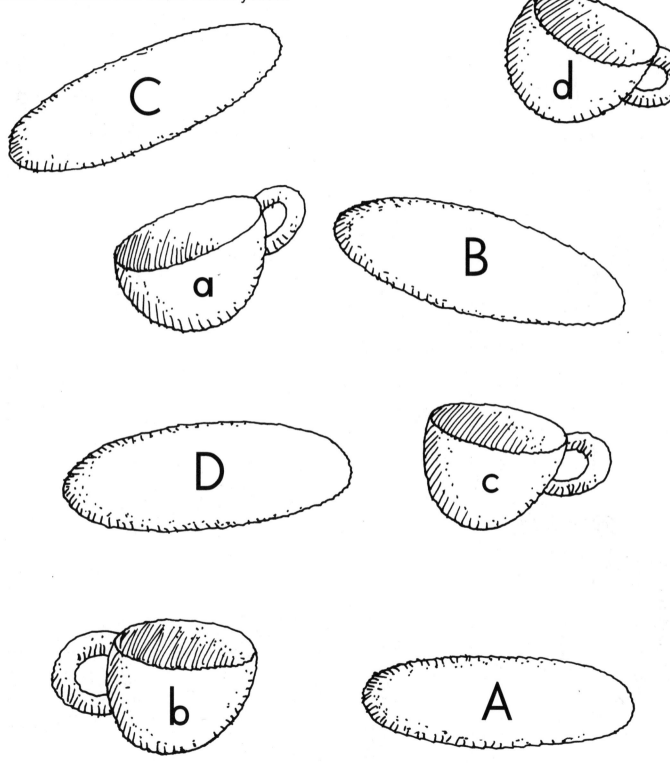

Skills: Ordering uppercase and lowercase letters; Following directions

ABC ORDER

Look at the uppercase and lowercase letters in the socks and shoes.
Color the ones that come first purple.
Color the ones that come second orange.
Color the ones that come third brown.
Color the ones that come fourth black.

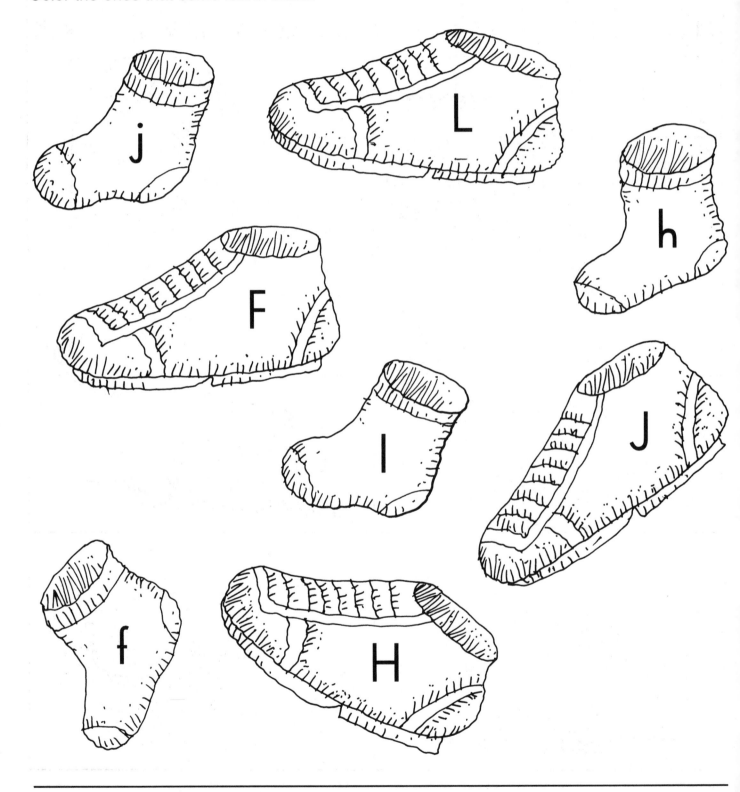

Skills: Ordering uppercase and lowercase letters; Following directions

ABC ORDER

Look at the alphabet at the top of the page.
Look at the pictures and words in the boxes.
Circle the first letter in each word.
Number the words from **1** to **6** to put them in alphabetical order.

a b c d e f g h i j k l m n o p q r s t u v w x y z

zebra

kite

cat

fox

nut

top

Skills: Using knowledge of letter order; Alphabetizing

ABC ORDER

Look at the alphabet at the top of the page.
Look at the pictures and words in the boxes.
Circle the first letter in each word.
Number the words from 1 to 6 to put them in alphabetical order.

a b c d e f g h i j k l m n o p q r s t u v w x y z

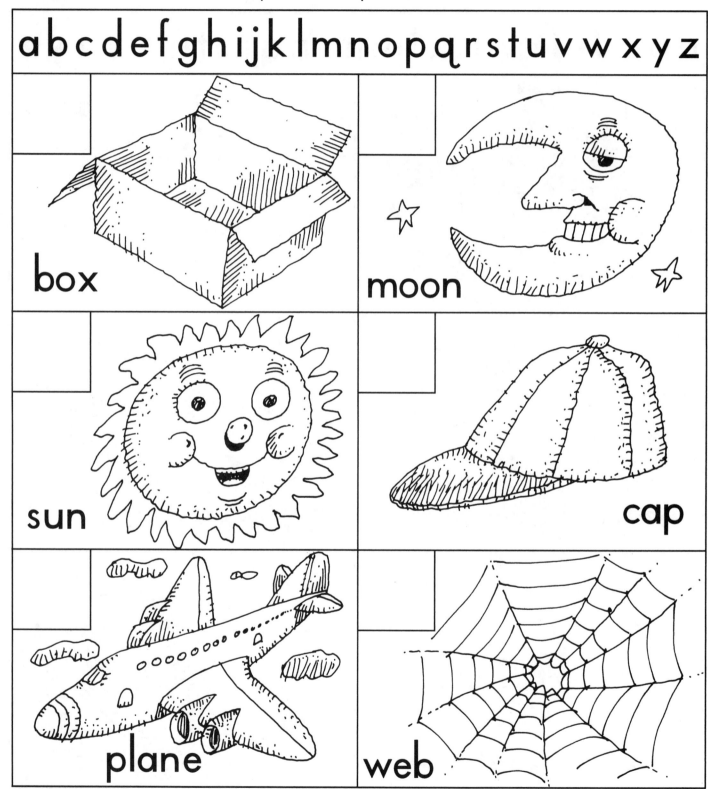

box

moon

sun

cap

plane

web

Skills: Using knowledge of letter order; Alphabetizing

ABC ORDER

Look at the alphabet at the top of the page.
Look at the pictures and words in the boxes.
Circle the first letter in each word.
Number the words from **I** to **6** to put them in alphabetical order.

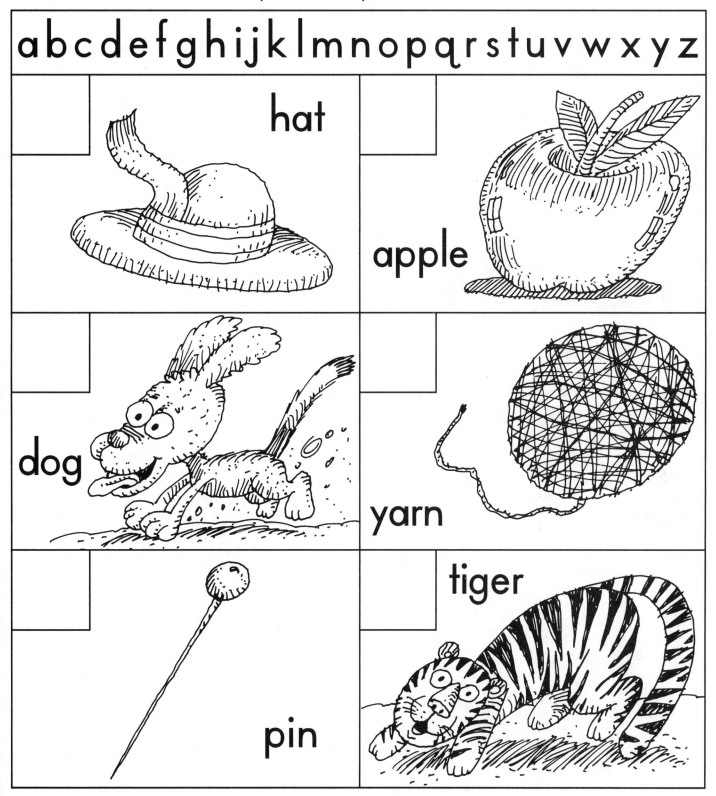

abcdefghijklmnopqrstuvwxyz

hat

apple

dog

yarn

pin

tiger

Skills: Using knowledge of letter order; Alphabetizing

ABC ORDER

Look at the alphabet at the top of the page.
Look at the pictures and words in the boxes.
Circle the first letter in each word.
Number the words from 1 to 6 to put them in alphabetical order.

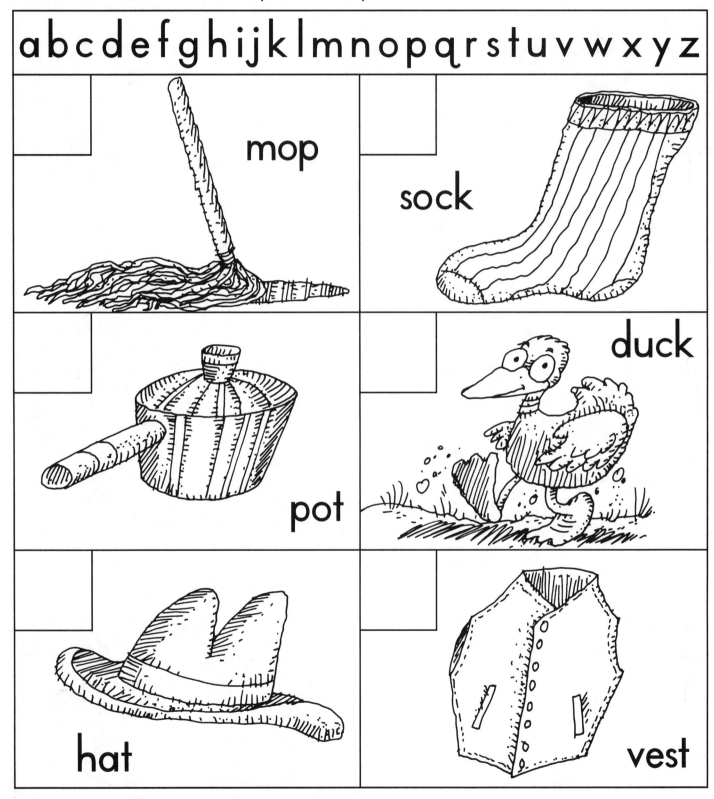

a b c d e f g h i j k l m n o p q r s t u v w x y z

mop

sock

pot

duck

hat

vest

Skills: Using knowledge of letter order; Alphabetizing

ABC ORDER

Look at the words in each piece of popcorn.
Look at the first letter of each word.
Circle the word that comes first in ABC order.

pie   lamp

lion   ring

ball   doll

sock   nut

bug   saw

hat   cake

Skills: Using knowledge of letter order; Alphabetizing skills

ABC ORDER

Look at the words in each book.
Look at the first letter of each word.
Circle the word that comes first in ABC order.

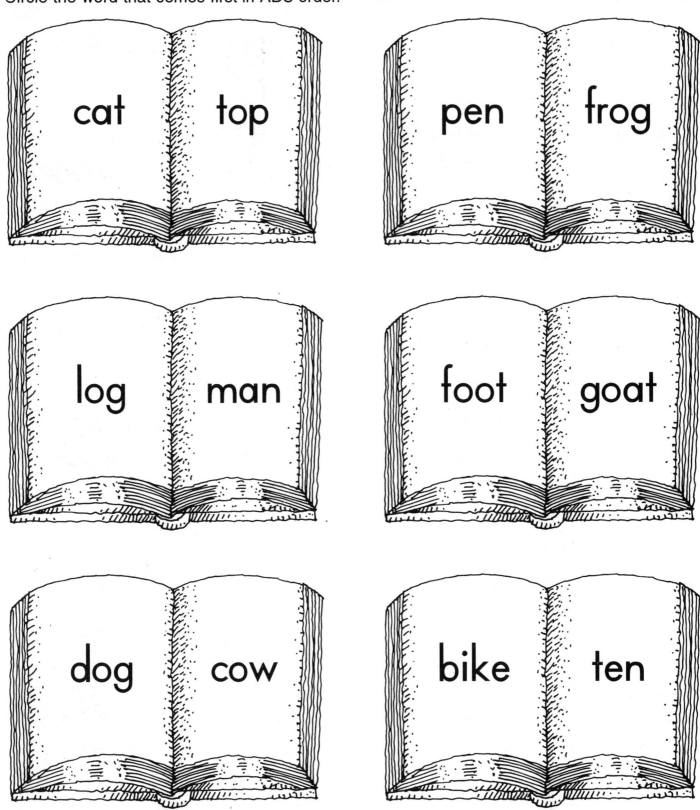

cat   top

pen   frog

log   man

foot   goat

dog   cow

bike   ten

Skills: Using knowledge of letter order; Alphabetizing skills

ABC ORDER

Look at the words in each balloon.
Look at the first letter of each word.
Circle the word that comes first in ABC order.

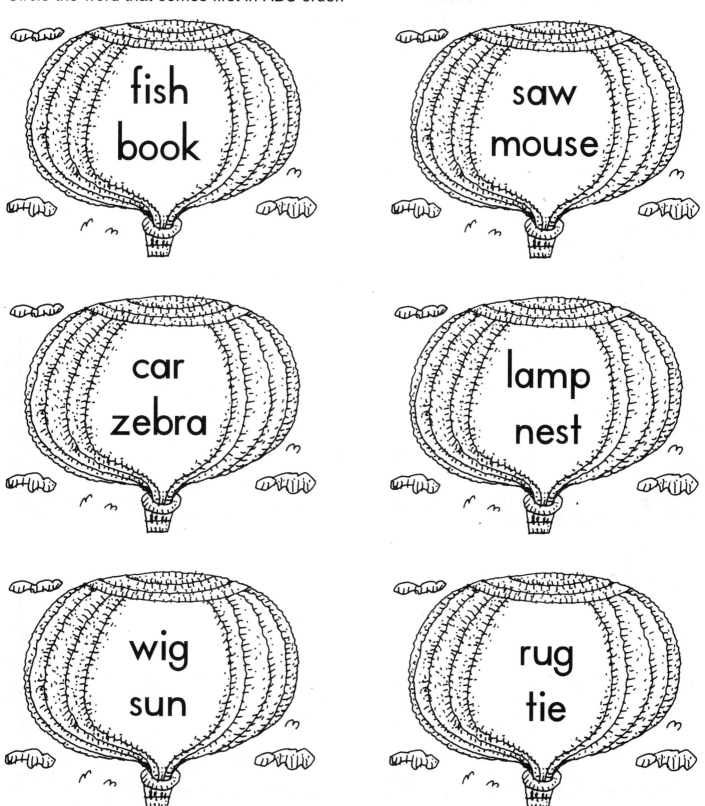

fish
book

saw
mouse

car
zebra

lamp
nest

wig
sun

rug
tie

Skills: Using knowledge of letter order; Alphabetizing

SHAPES AND COLORS

Look at the shape at the top of the page.
Look at the shapes in the column below it.
Color the shape in each column that goes with the one at the top.

Skills: Shape recognition; Visual discrimination; Fine motor skill development

SHAPES AND COLORS

Look at the shape at the top of the page.
Look at the shapes in the column below it.
Color the shape in each column that goes with the one at the top.

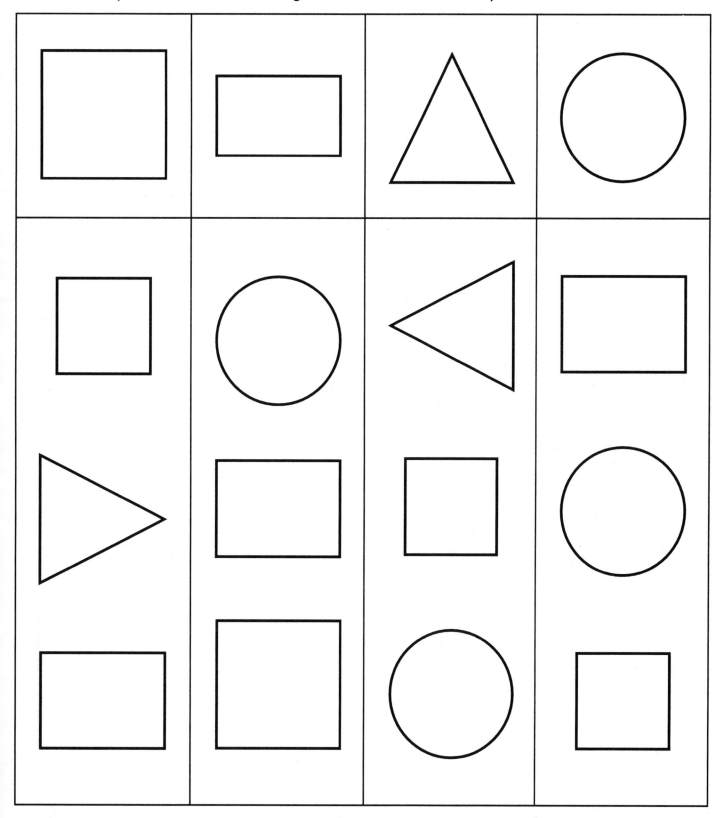

Skills: Shape recognition; Visual discrimination; Fine motor skill development

SHAPES AND COLORS

Look at the word **circle** at the top of the page.
Trace and then write the word.
Look at the shapes in the box below.
Color the circles.

circle

Skills: Shape and shape word recognition; Visual discrimination; Fine motor skill development

SHAPES AND COLORS

Look at the circle and the word **circle** in the center of the page.
Look at the words that are scattered around it.
Draw a line under the word **circle** each time it appears.

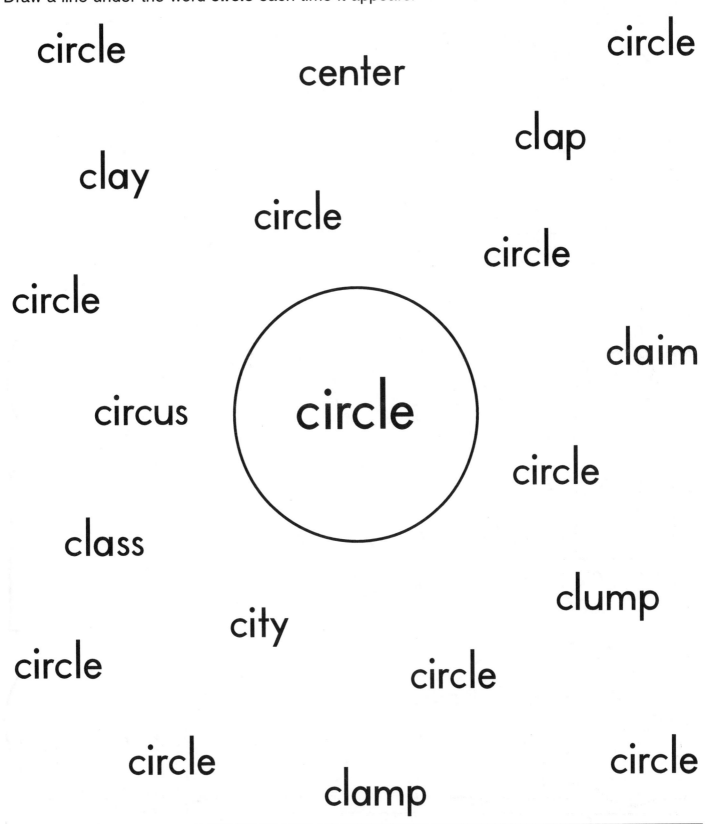

circle   center   circle

clap

clay   circle

circle

circle

claim

circus   circle

circle

class

clump

city

circle   circle

circle   circle

clamp

Skills: Shape and shape word recognition; Visual discrimination

SHAPES AND COLORS

Help the shape man get home.
Follow the path with the word **circle** and pictures of circles through the maze.
It will lead to his home.

Skills: Shape and shape word recognition; Fine motor skill development

SHAPES AND COLORS

Look at the word **square** at the top of the page.
Trace and then write the word.
Look at the shapes in the box below.
Color the squares.

square

Skills: Shape and shape word recognition; Visual discrimination; Fine motor skill
development

SHAPES AND COLORS

Look at the word **square** at the top of the page.
Trace and then write that word.
Trace the squares in the box below.
Then draw your own squares.

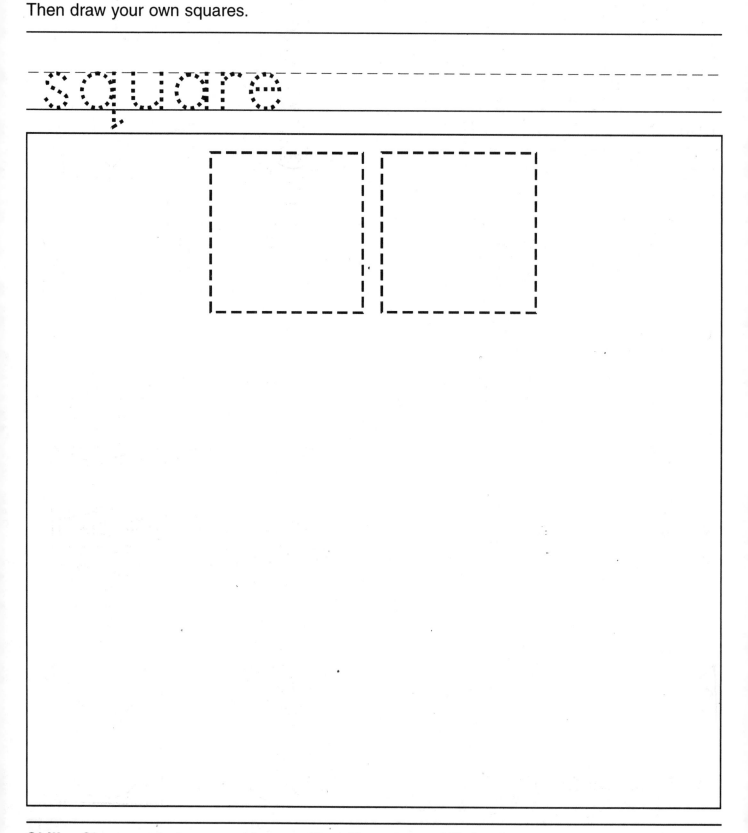

Skills: Shape and shape word recognition; Fine motor skill development

SHAPES AND COLORS

The shape man wants to take a train ride.
Follow the path with the word **square** and pictures of squares through the maze.
It will lead to the train.

Skills: Shape and shape word recognition; Fine motor skill development

SHAPES AND COLORS

Look at the word **triangle** at the top of the page.
Trace and then write the word.
Look at the shapes in the box below.
Color the triangles.

triangle

Skills: Shape and shape word recognition; Visual discrimination; Fine motor skill development

SHAPES AND COLORS

Look at the triangle and the word **triangle** in the center of the page.
Look at the words that are scattered around it.
Draw a line under the word **triangle** each time it appears.

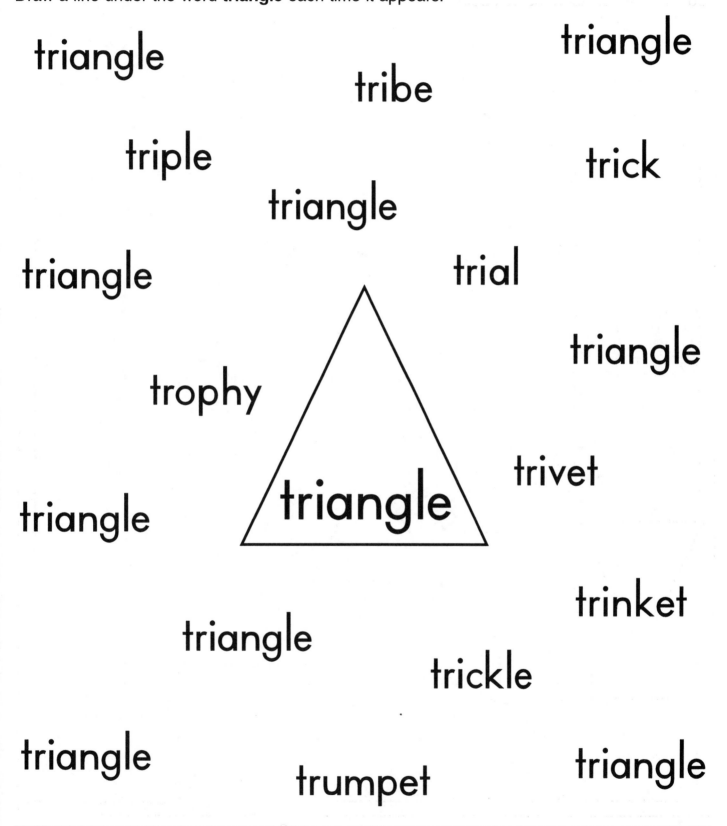

triangle

triangle

tribe

triple

trick

triangle

triangle

trial

trophy

triangle

triangle

trivet

triangle

trinket

triangle

trickle

triangle

trumpet

triangle

Skills: Shape and shape word recognition; Visual discrimination

SHAPES AND COLORS

The shape man is going for a boat ride.
Follow the path with the word **triangle** and pictures of triangles through the maze.
It will lead to the boat.

Skills: Shape and shape word recognition; Fine motor skill development

SHAPES AND COLORS

Look at the word **rectangle** at the top of the page.
Trace and then write the word.
Look at the shapes in the box below.
Color the rectangles.

rectangle

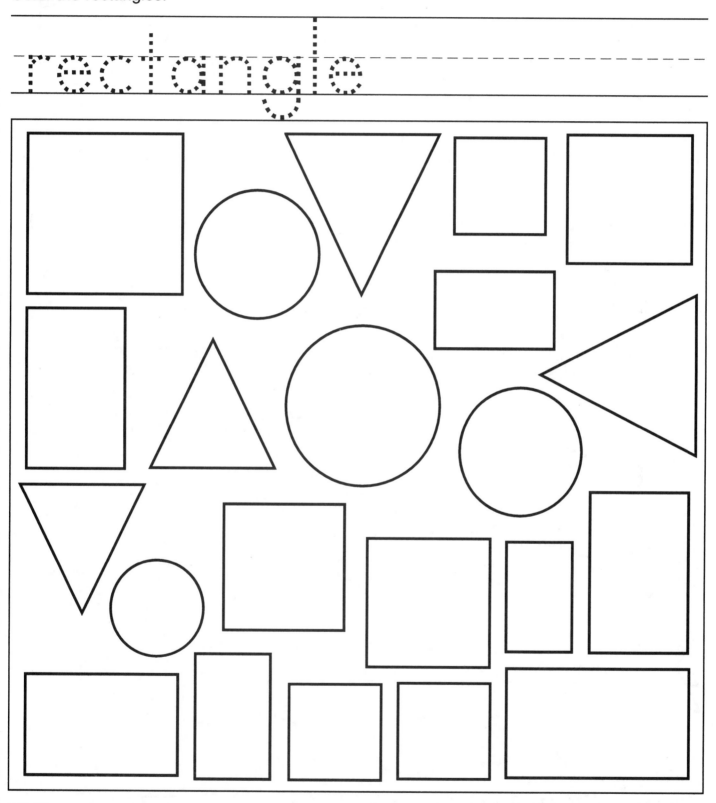

Skills: Shape and shape word recognition; Visual discrimination; Fine motor skill development

SHAPES AND COLORS

It's time for the shape man to catch an airplane.
Follow the path with the word **rectangle** and pictures of rectangles through the maze.
It will lead to his airplane.

Skills: Shape and shape word recognition; Fine motor skill development

SHAPES AND COLORS

Look at the words on the left.
Look at the pictures on the right.
Draw lines to match the pictures and words that go together.
Then draw these four shapes in the box at the bottom of the page.

circle

triangle

rectangle

square

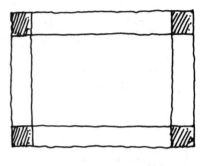

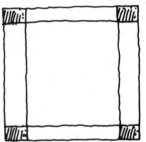

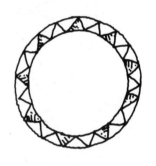

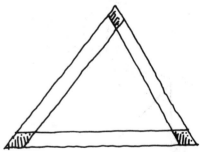

Skills: Shape and shape word recognition; Fine motor skill development

SHAPES AND COLORS

Look at the word **red** at the top of the page.
Trace and then write the word.
Which pictures should be red? Color them.

red

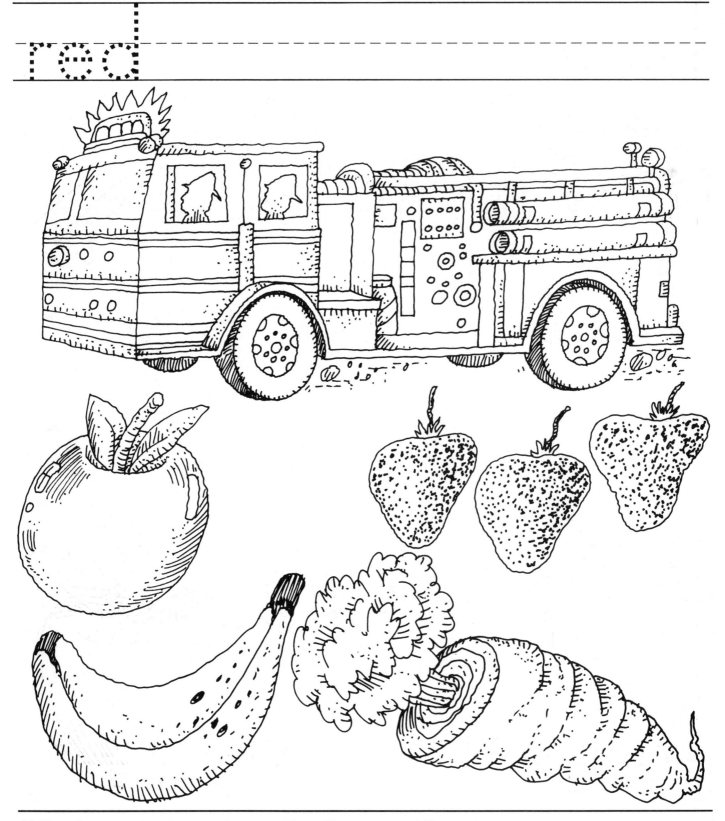

Skills: Color and color word recognition; Fine motor skill development

SHAPES AND COLORS

Look at the word **blue** at the top of the page.
Trace and then write the word.
Which pictures should be blue? Color them.

blue

Skills: Color and color word recognition; Fine motor skill development

SHAPES AND COLORS

Look at the word **yellow** at the top of the page.
Trace and then write the word.
Which pictures should be yellow? Color them.

yellow

Skills: Color and color word recognition; Fine motor skill development

SHAPES AND COLORS

Look at the word **green** at the top of the page.
Trace and then write the word.
Which pictures should be green? Color them.

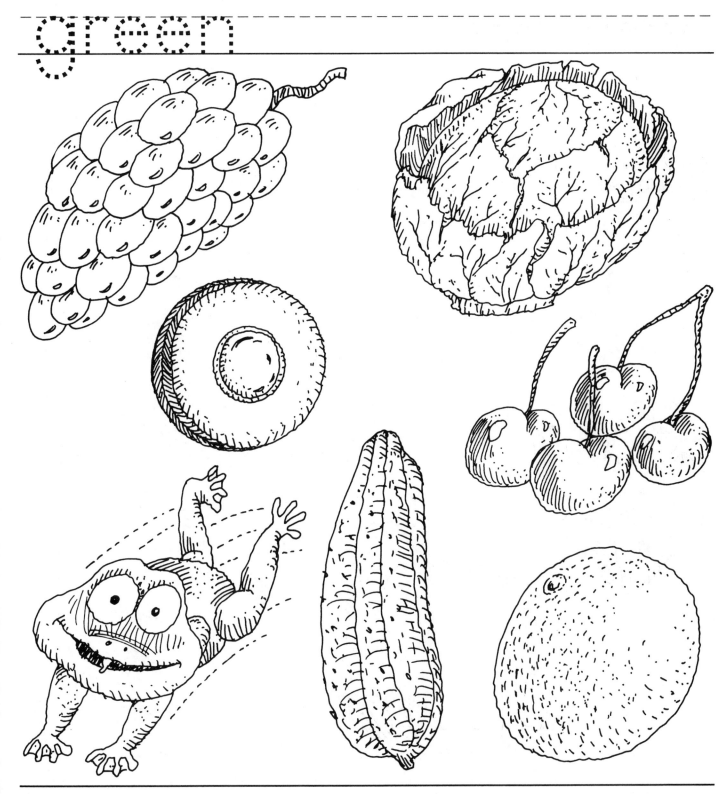

Skills: Color and color word recognition; Fine motor skill development

SHAPES AND COLORS

Look at the word **orange** at the top of the page.
Trace and then write the word.
Which pictures should be orange? Color them.

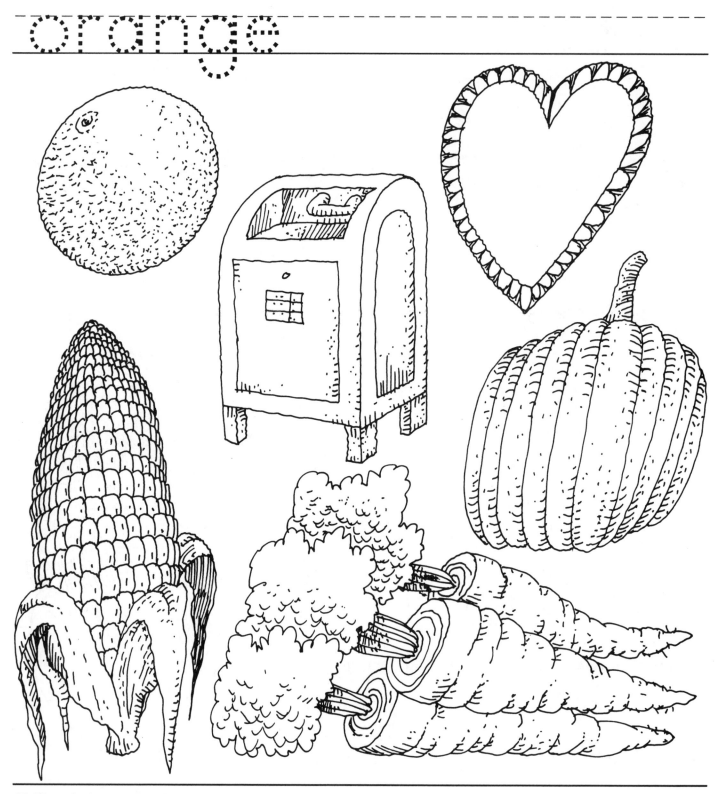

orange

Skills: Color and color word recognition; Fine motor skill development

SHAPES AND COLORS

Look at the word **purple** at the top of the page.
Trace and then write the word.
Which pictures should be purple? Color them.

purple

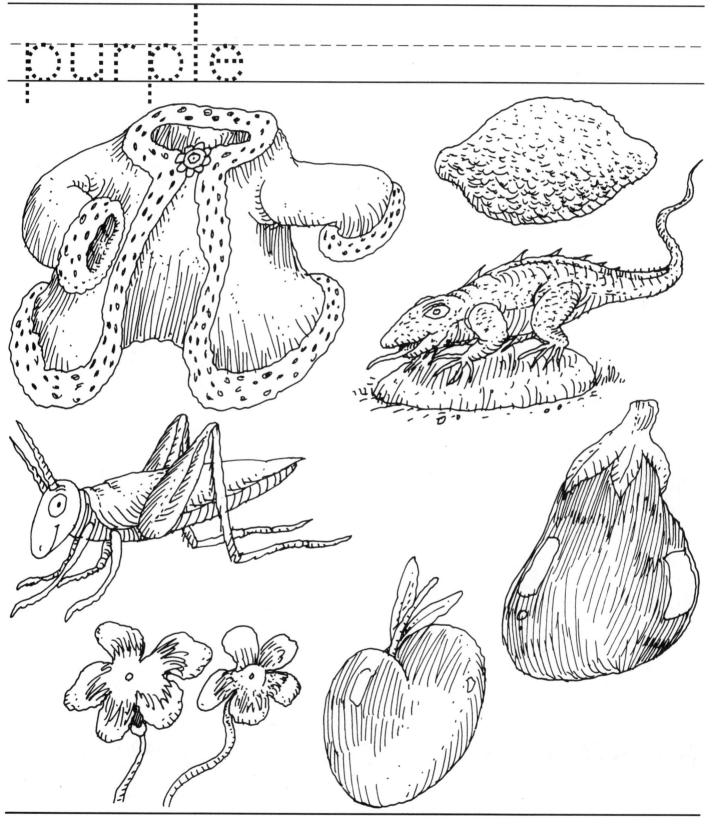

Skills: Color and color word recognition; Fine motor skill development

SHAPES AND COLORS

Look at the word **brown** at the top of the page.
Trace and then write the word.
Which pictures should be brown? Color them.

brown

Skills: Color and color word recognition; Fine motor skill development

SHAPES AND COLORS

Look at the word **black** at the top of the page.
Trace and then write the word.
Which pictures should be black? Color them.

black

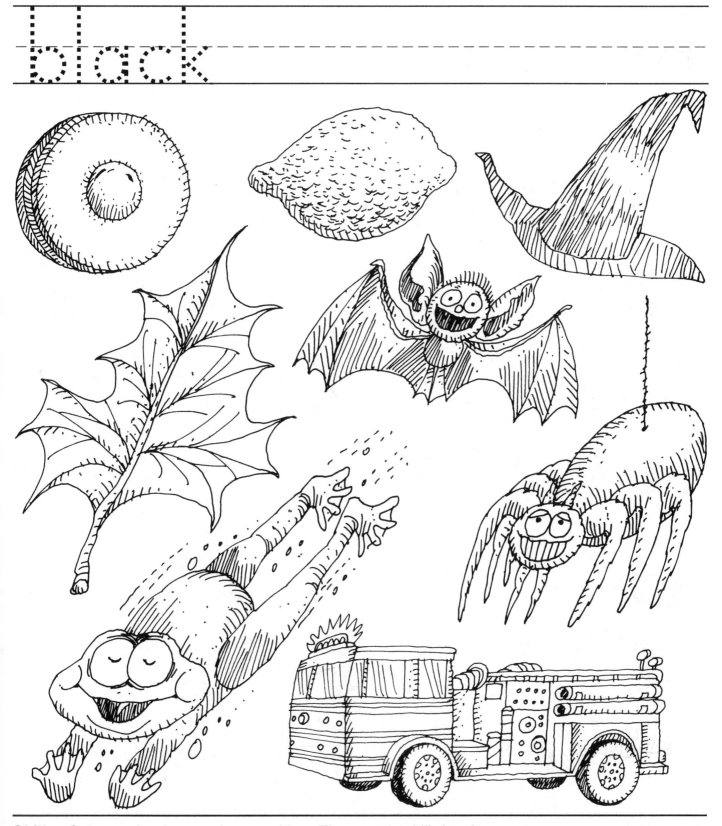

Skills: Color and color word recognition; Fine motor skill development

SHAPES AND COLORS

Look at the word **pink** at the top of the page.
Trace and then write the word.
Which pictures should be pink? Color them.

pink

Skills: Color and color word recognition; Fine motor skill development

SHAPES AND COLORS

Look at the picture in each box.
Finish the pictures by following the directions in each box.

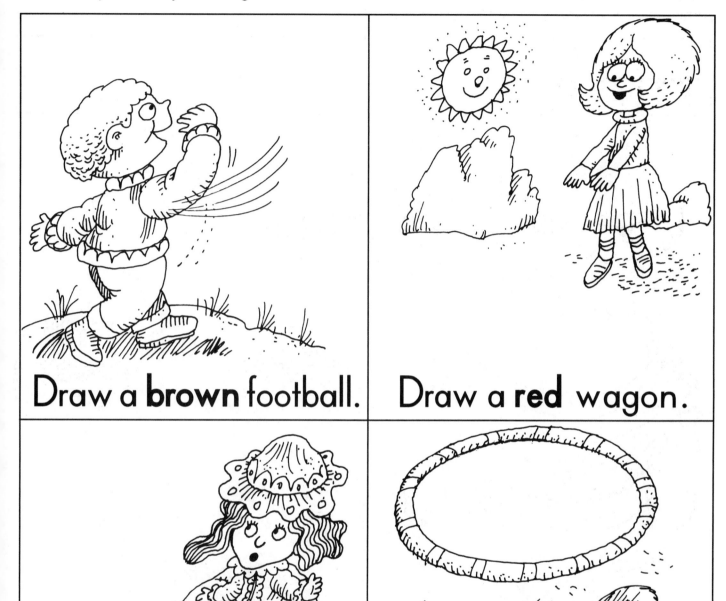

Draw a **brown** football.

Draw a **red** wagon.

Draw a **black** spider.

Draw **yellow** cheese.

Skills: Color word recognition; Following directions

SHAPES AND COLORS

Look at the picture in each box.
Finish the pictures by following the directions in each box.

Draw a **blue** bird.

Draw a **green** frog.

Draw an **orange** pumpkin.

Draw **purple** grapes.

Skills: Color word recognition; Following directions

SHAPES AND COLORS

What a funny clown!
Look at the color word in each section.
Color each part to match the color word.

Skills: Color word recognition; Fine motor skill development

SHAPES AND COLORS

Look at the picture below and follow the directions.
Color the apples in the basket red. Color the bananas yellow.
Color the boy's jacket blue. Color the lettuce green.
Color the carrots orange. Color the girl's dress purple.

Skills: Following directions; Color word recognition; Fine motor skill development

SHAPES AND COLORS

Who is hiding in this picture?
Follow the directions to find out.
Color the **A** spaces red. Color the **B** spaces blue.
Color the **C** spaces yellow. Color the **D** spaces green.
Color the **E** spaces purple. Color the **F** spaces orange.

Skills: Distinguishing color; Following color codes; Fine motor skill development

SHAPES AND COLORS

Look at the race cars going around the track.
Color each car to match the color word.
Then color the track black.

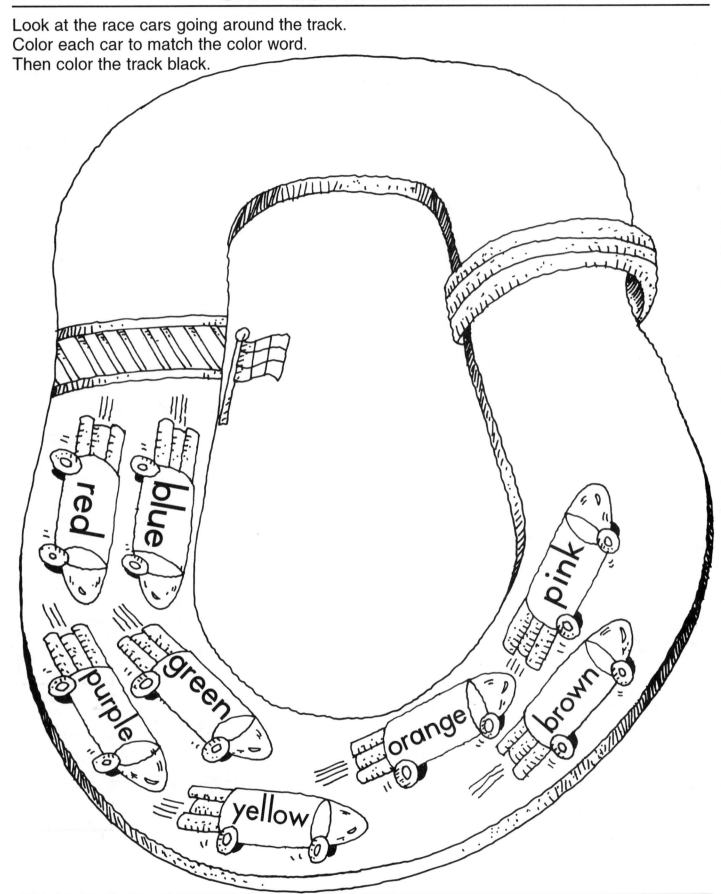

Skills: Color and color word recognition; Fine motor skill development

SHAPES AND COLORS

Look at the words on the left.
Look at the words and boxes on the right.
Draw lines to match the pairs of words that are alike.
Then color each box to match the word next to it.

pink   blue   ☐

green   red   ☐

red   brown   ☐

blue   green   ☐

brown   pink   ☐

Skills: Color and color word recognition; Fine motor skill development

SHAPES AND COLORS

Look at the shapes at the top of the page.
Look at the words in each box below.
Draw the corresponding shape in each box.
Color each shape the named color.

circle

red

rectangle

blue

square

green

triangle

yellow

Skills: Color and shape word recognition; Fine motor skill development

WORDS ABOUT NUMBERS

Look at the word **one** at the top of the page.
Trace and then write the word.
Then color the pictures that show sets of one.

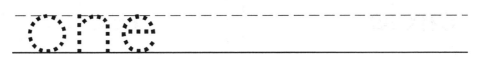

Skills: Number and number word recognition; Fine motor skill development

WORDS ABOUT NUMBERS

Look at the word **two** at the top of the page.
Trace and then write the word.
Then color the pictures that show sets of two.

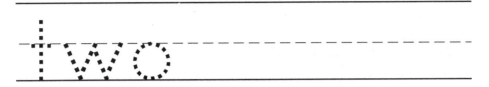

Skills: Number and number word recognition; Fine motor skill development

WORDS ABOUT NUMBERS

Look at the word **three** at the top of the page.
Trace and then write the word.
Then color the pictures that show sets of three.

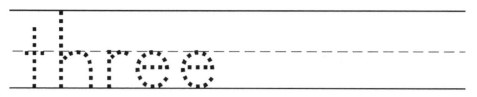

Skills: Number and number word recognition; Fine motor skill development

WORDS ABOUT NUMBERS

Look at the word **four** at the top of the page.
Trace and then write the word.
Then color the pictures that show sets of four.

Skills: Number and number word recognition; Fine motor skill development

WORDS ABOUT NUMBERS

Look at the word **five** at the top of the page.
Trace and then write the word.
Then color the pictures that show sets of five.

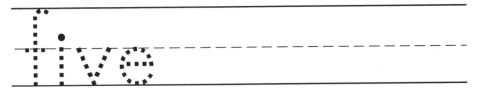

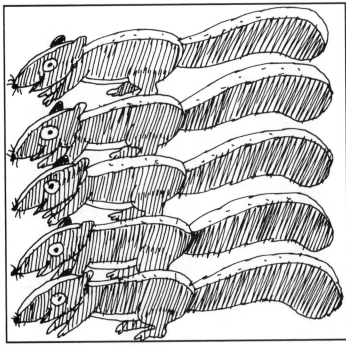

Skills: Number and number word recognition; Fine motor skill development

WORDS ABOUT NUMBERS

Look at the word **six** at the top of the page.
Trace and then write the word.
Then color the pictures that show sets of six.

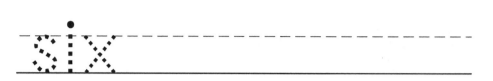

Skills: Number and number word recognition; Fine motor skill development

WORDS ABOUT NUMBERS

Look at the word **seven** at the top of the page.
Trace and then write the word.
Then color the pictures that show sets of seven.

Skills: Number and number word recognition; Fine motor skill development

WORDS ABOUT NUMBERS

Look at the word **eight** at the top of the page.
Trace and then write the word.
Then color the pictures that show sets of eight.

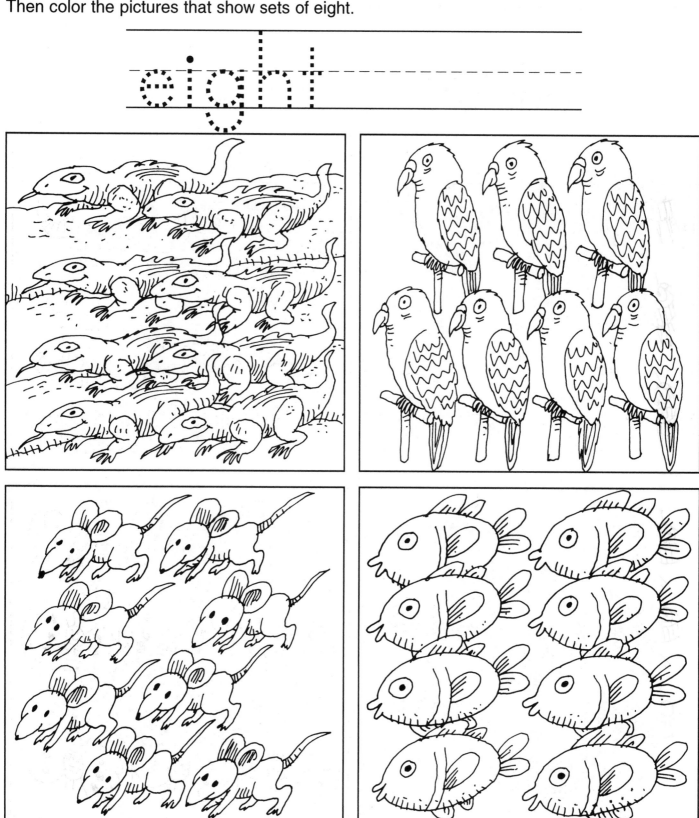

Skills: Number and number word recognition; Fine motor skill development

WORDS ABOUT NUMBERS

Look at the word **nine** at the top of the page.
Trace and then write the word.
Then color the pictures that show sets of nine.

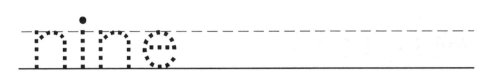

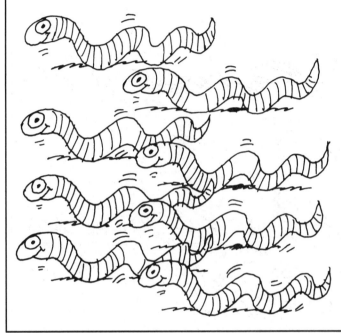

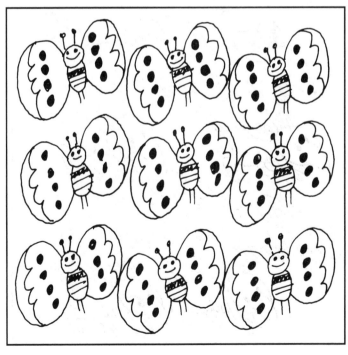

Skills: Number and number word recognition; Fine motor skill development

WORDS ABOUT NUMBERS

Look at the word **ten** at the top of the page.
Trace and then write the word.
Then color the pictures that show sets of ten.

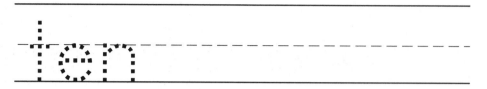

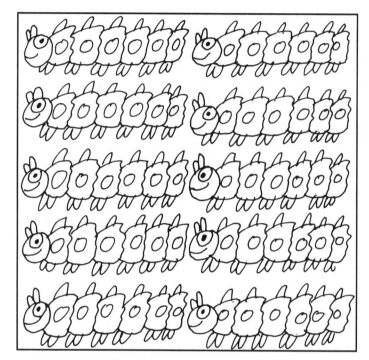

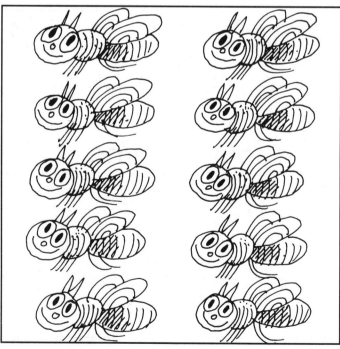

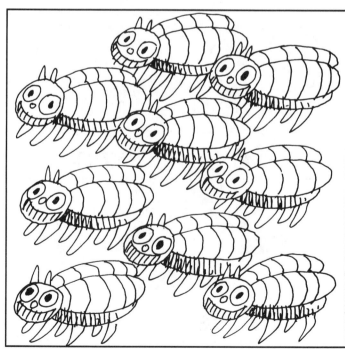

Skills: Number and number word recognition; Fine motor skill development

WORDS ABOUT NUMBERS

Look at the picture in each box.
Circle the word that tells how many.

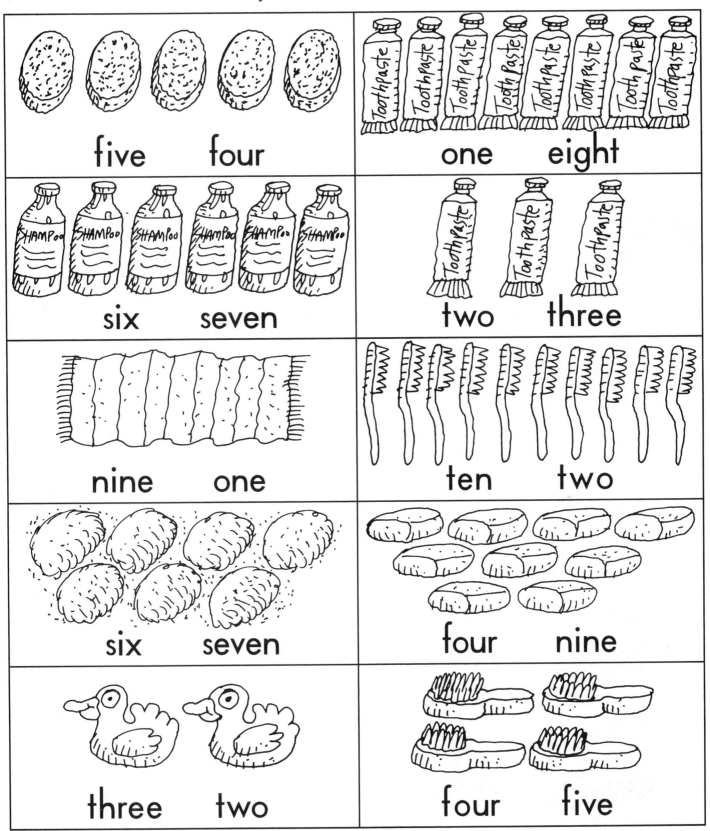

five   four

one   eight

six   seven

two   three

nine   one

ten   two

six   seven

four   nine

three   two

four   five

Skills: Number word recognition; Following directions

WORDS ABOUT NUMBERS

Look at the number at the beginning of each row.
Circle the matching number word in each row.

4	five four one
3	three two five
1	four three one
5	two five four
2	three four two

Skills: Number word recognition; Matching numerals and number words

WORDS ABOUT NUMBERS

Look at the number at the beginning of each row.
Circle the matching number word in each row.

7	six seven ten
9	eight six nine
6	six eight seven
10	ten seven eight
8	ten eight nine

Skills: Number word recognition; Matching numerals and number words

VOCABULARY BUILDING

Look at the words at the top of the page.
Say each word aloud.
Trace each word below.
Then color the pictures and read each picture-word sentence.

a

the

There is a  on the .

Skills: Building vocabulary vond spelling words; Learning sight vocabulary; Fine motor skill development

290

VOCABULARY BUILDING

Look at the words at the top of the page.
Say each word aloud.
Trace each word below.
Then color the pictures and read each picture-word sentence.

The ___ is on the ___ .

The ___ is off the ___ .

Skills: Building vocabulary vond spelling words; Learning sight vocabulary; Fine motor skill development

VOCABULARY BUILDING

Look at the words at the top of the page.
Say each word aloud.
Trace each word below.
Then color the pictures and read each picture-word sentence.

in

out

in

out

The [picture] is in the [picture].

The [picture] is out of the [picture].

Skills: Building vocabulary vond spelling words; Learning sight vocabulary; Fine motor skill development

292

VOCABULARY BUILDING

Look at the words at the top of the page.
Say each word aloud.
Trace each word below.
Then color the pictures and read each picture-word sentence.

up

down

up

down

The 🏴 is up the .

The 🏴 is down the .

Skills: Building vocabulary vond spelling words; Learning sight vocabulary; Fine motor skill development

VOCABULARY BUILDING

Look at the words at the top of the page.
Say each word aloud.
Trace each word below.
Then color the pictures and read each picture-word sentence.

over

under

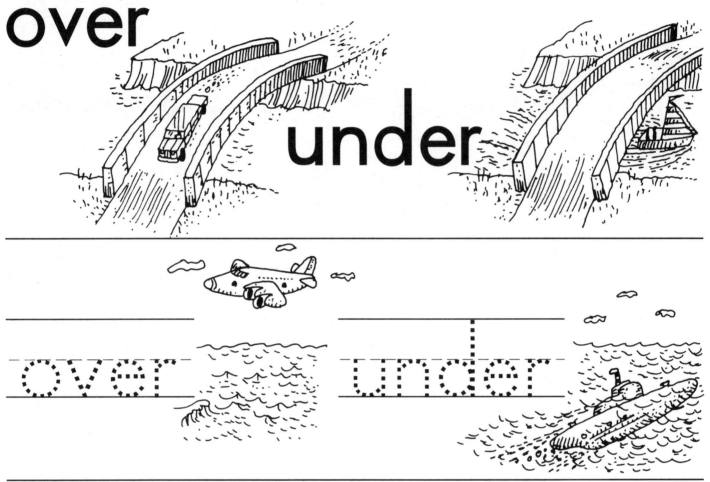

The 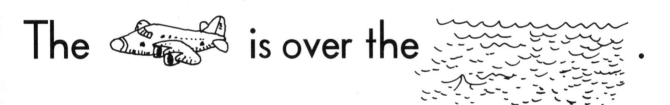 is over the _____ .

The 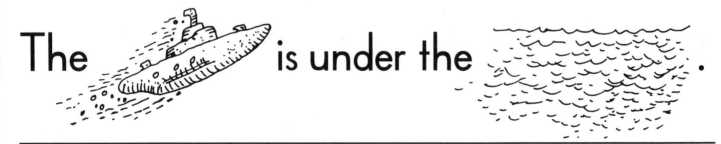 is under the _____ .

Skills: Building vocabulary vond spelling words; Learning sight vocabulary; Fine motor skill development

VOCABULARY BUILDING

Look at the words at the top of the page.
Say each word aloud.
Trace each word below.
Then color the pictures and read each picture-word sentence.

happy

sad

The ___ is happy.

The ___ is sad.

Skills: Building vocabulary vond spelling words; Learning sight vocabulary; Fine motor skill development

VOCABULARY BUILDING

Look at the words at the top of the page.
Say each word aloud.
Trace each word below.
Then color the pictures and read each picture-word sentence.

big

little

big

little

The _____ is big.

The _____ is little.

Skills: Building vocabulary vnd spelling words; Learning sight vocabulary; Fine motor skill development

VOCABULARY BUILDING

Look at the words and pictures at the top of the page.
Trace each word.
Look at the words and pictures at the bottom of the page.
Draw lines to match the words and pictures.
Then color the pictures.

bird   cat   dog   fish

Skills: Building vocabulary vond spelling words; Learning sight vocabulary; Fine motor skill development

VOCABULARY BUILDING

Look at the words and pictures at the top of the page.
Trace each word.
Look at the words and pictures at the bottom of the page.
Draw lines to match the words and pictures.
Then color the pictures.

_____

cow

_____

horse

sheep

pig

horse   pig   cow   sheep

Skills: Building vocabulary vand spelling words; Learning sight vocabulary; Fine motor skill development

298

VOCABULARY BUILDING

Look at the words and pictures at the top of the page.
Trace each word.
Look at the words and pictures at the bottom of the page.
Draw lines to match the words and pictures.
Then color the pictures.

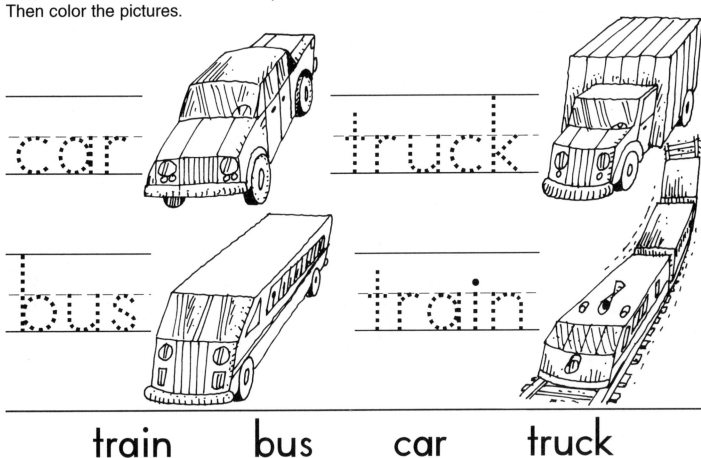

train   bus   car   truck

Skills: Building vocabulary vond spelling words; Learning sight vocabulary; Fine motor skill development

VOCABULARY BUILDING

Look at the words and pictures at the top of the page.
Trace each word.
Look at the words and pictures at the bottom of the page.
Draw lines to match the words and pictures.
Then color the pictures.

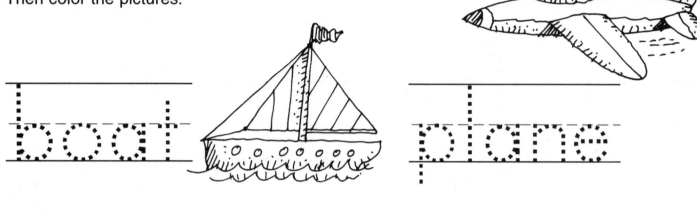

boat

plane

cab

bike

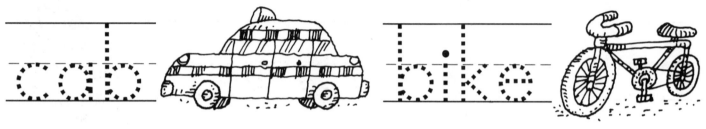

plane   boat   bike   cab

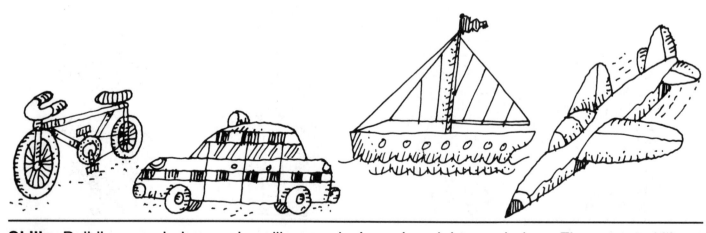

Skills: Building vocabulary vnd spelling words; Learning sight vocabulary; Fine motor skill development

300

VOCABULARY BUILDING

Look at the words and pictures at the top of the page.
Trace each word.
Look at the words and pictures at the bottom of the page.
Draw lines to match the words and pictures.
Then color the pictures.

man   girl   boy   woman

Skills: Building vocabulary vond spelling words; Learning sight vocabulary; Fine motor skill development

VOCABULARY BUILDING

Look at the words and pictures at the top of the page.
Trace each word.
Look at the words and pictures at the bottom of the page.
Draw lines to match the words and pictures.
Then color the pictures.

cup   spoon   fork   plate

Skills: Building vocabulary vand spelling words; Learning sight vocabulary; Fine motor skill development

VOCABULARY BUILDING

Look at the picture and word at the beginning of each row.
Then look at the rest of the words in each row.
Circle the word that matches the first word.

paint	throw paint brush
throw	jump fly throw
dig	swing brush dig
fly	fly dig hop

Skills: Building vocabulary vond spelling words; Learning sight vocabulary; Visual discrimination

COMPREHENSION

Read each sentence.
Then look at the pictures beside it.
Follow the directions in the sentence.

Color the nest.

Circle the sheep.

Circle the big bee.

Color the bear brown.

Skills: Using comprehension skills to follow directions; Recognizing spelling words and sight vocabulary

COMPREHENSION

Read each sentence.
Then look at the pictures beside it.
Follow the directions in the sentence.

Draw a log under the frog.

Color the small hat.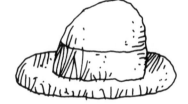

Circle three fish.

Color the boat orange.

Skills: Using comprehension skills to follow directions; Recognizing spelling words and sight vocabulary

COMPREHENSION

Read each sentence.
Then look at the pictures beside it.
Follow the directions from the sentence.

Draw a book on the table.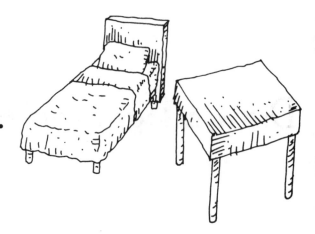

Draw a line over the turtle.

Color the fox brown.

Circle the moon.

Skills: Using comprehension skills to follow directions; Recognizing spelling words and sight vocabulary

COMPREHENSION

Read each sentence.
Then look at the pictures beside it.
Follow the directions from the sentence.

Draw a star near the moon.

Draw a cloud under the sun.

Circle the little mouse.

Color the flower orange.

Skills: Using comprehension skills to follow directions; Recognizing spelling words and sight vocabulary

COMPREHENSION

Read the words in the box at the top of the page.
Then read each sentence.
Add the missing word from the box at the top.

hat	read	car	fish

The _____ can swim.

The _____ has four wheels.

Put on your _____ .

The girl likes to _____ .

Skills: Using context clues to complete sentences; Recognizing spelling words and sight vocabulary; Fine motor skill development

COMPREHENSION

Read the words in the box at the top of the page.
Then read each sentence.
Add the missing word from the box at the top.

plane	dress	chair	bike

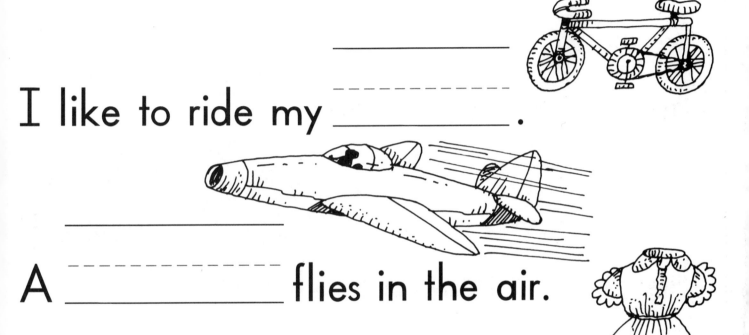

I like to ride my _____ .

A _____ flies in the air.

The girl put on a red _____ .

You can sit on a _____ .

Skills: Using context clues to complete sentences; Recognizing spelling words and sight vocabulary; Fine motor skill development

COMPREHENSION

Read the words in the box at the top of the page.
Then read each sentence.
Add the missing word from the box at the top.

boy	swing	funny	fork

The clown was _____ .

The _____ went to sleep.

You eat with a _____ .

The girl was on a _____ .

Skills: Using context clues to complete sentences; Recognizing spelling words and sight vocabulary; Fine motor skill development

COMPREHENSION

Read the words in the box at the top of the page.
Then read each sentence.
Add the missing word from the box at the top.

walk	under	coat	throw

We sat _____ the tree.

The boy had a green _____ .

We can _____ to school.

He can _____ the ball.

Skills: Using context clues to complete sentences; Recognizing spelling words and sight vocabulary; Fine motor skill development

COMPREHENSION

Read the words in the box at the top of the page.
Then read each sentence.
Add the missing word from the box at the top.

doll	shirt	cab	cat

She plays with a pretty _____ .

We rode in a yellow _____ .

Put on your blue _____ .

The _____ ran up a tree.

Skills: Using context clues to complete sentences; Recognizing spelling words and sight vocabulary; Fine motor skill development

COMPREHENSION

Read the words in the box at the top of the page.
Then read each sentence.
Add the missing word from the box at the top.

head	ball	jump	horse

The boy caught the _____ .

I stood on my _____ .

She rode a _____ .

Let's _____ rope.

Skills: Using context clues to complete sentences; Recognizing spelling words and sight vocabulary; Fine motor skill development

COMPREHENSION

Read the sentence in each box.
Draw a picture of what it says.

I see the moon and the stars.

The boy can climb a tree.

The duck is yellow.

Look at that red car.

Skills: Using comprehension skills to follow directions; Recognizing spelling words and sight vocabulary; Fine motor skill development

COMPREHENSION

Look at the blue
cup and plate.

The boy can read
a book.

That is a big flower.

I see three fish.

Skills: Using comprehension skills to follow directions; Recognizing spelling words and sight vocabulary; Fine motor skill development

COMPREHENSION

The block is on the table.

That is a big bear.

The girl has a bat and ball.

Look at the brown cow.

Skills: Using comprehension skills to follow directions; Recognizing spelling words and sight vocabulary; Fine motor skill development

COMPREHENSION

Read the sentence in each box.
Draw a picture of what it says.

Look at the green turtle.

I see the yellow sun.

I have a red cup.

That is a big truck.

Skills: Using comprehension skills to follow directions; Recognizing spelling words and sight vocabulary; Fine motor skill development

COMPREHENSION

Read the sentence in each box.
Draw a picture of what it says.

I use the purple
fork and spoon.

I see two hands.

Go brush your teeth.

We will ride
the train.

Skills: Using comprehension skills to follow directions; Recognizing spelling words and sight vocabulary; Fine motor skill development

COMPREHENSION

Look at the picture below.
Read the sentences.
Follow the directions to add to the picture.

Draw two green trees.
Add one swing.
Draw a girl on the slide.
Add some blue flowers.

Skills: Using comprehension skills to follow directions; Recognizing spelling words and sight vocabulary; Fine motor skill development

COMPREHENSION

Look at the picture below.
Read the sentences.
Follow the directions to add to the picture.

Draw a cow in the grass.
Draw a duck in the pond.
Draw a horse near the barn.
Draw a pig in the pen.

Skills: Using comprehension skills to follow directions; Recognizing spelling words and sight vocabulary; Fine motor skill development